FINDING RICHARD III

The Official Account
of Research by the Retrieval and Reburial Project

FINDING RICHARD III

The Official Account
of Research
by the Retrieval and Reburial Project

together with original materials and documentation

A.J. Carson (Ed.),
J. Ashdown-Hill, D. Johnson, W. Johnson
& P.J. Langley

Imprimis
Imprimatur

Also by Annette Carson:
Flight Unlimited (with Eric Müller)
Flight Unlimited '95 (with Eric Müller)
Flight Fantastic: The Illustrated History of Aerobatics
Jeff Beck: Crazy Fingers
Richard III: The Maligned King
Richard III: A Small Guide to the Great Debate

Also by John Ashdown-Hill:
Eleanor, the Secret Queen
Mediaeval Colchester's Lost Landmarks
Richard III's 'Beloved Cousyn': John Howard and the House of York
The Last Days of Richard III
Royal Marriage Secrets: Consorts & Concubines Bigamists & Bastards
The Third Plantagenet, George, Duke of Clarence, Brother of Richard III

Also by David Johnson:
Adwalton Moor 1643: The Battle that Changed a War

Also by Philippa Langley:
The King's Grave: The Search for Richard III (with Michael Jones)

Published by Imprimis Imprimatur
21 Havergate, Horstead, NR12 7EJ
email@annettecarson.plus.com

British Library Cataloguing in Publication Data.
A catalogue record for this book is available from the British Library.

ISBN 978-0-9576840-2-7

Printed/bound in England by Barnwell Print, Dunkirk, Aylsham, NR11 6SU

Contents

Preface

Students of the late 15th century have more than their fair share of gripping historical mysteries to consider, among them an unsolved mediaeval "whodunnit" (the fate of the 'Princes in the Tower'), several princely claimants of uncertain origin (precisely who were Lambert Simnel and Perkin Warbeck?) and, until very recently, the last resting place of Richard III. Indeed, Richard's own political life, his short-lived but eventful rule and his demise in battle against Henry Tudor at Bosworth in 1485, continues to fascinate. In 2009 the possibility of finding Richard's remains, and adding significantly to our knowledge of his life, death and reputation, brought together a group of independent historical researchers and writers, in the *Looking For Richard Project*. Led by Philippa Langley, they shared membership of the Richard III Society and many years of prior independent study on the subject. This book is the authoritative, and frequently gripping, account of their discovery of the king's last resting place. It is written by the same team who organised the project, made the key historical and genealogical findings, and assembled the funding for the archaeological excavation.

The team's historical detective work involved painstaking re-consideration of all the sources for his burial and tomb, confirming its location in the choir of the Franciscan Priory in Leicester. But where was the choir? Here the team's scholarly analysis of Leicester's late mediaeval urban topography and of the layout of mendicant friaries had to overcome not only the errors made by later antiquaries and traditions, but also had to face down a persistent lack of 'professional' enthusiasm about their research. Yet locating a skeleton was never likely to be enough – only if Richard III's DNA could be traced forward in time to living relatives could his remains be identified beyond all doubt. John Ashdown-Hill's genealogical research was pivotal in establishing one such a line of descent and demonstrating that mtDNA could be available from living descendants of Richard's female siblings.

The *Looking For Richard Project* culminated in a specially commissioned archaeological investigation. One can only admire Philippa Langley's persistence in finding financial backers, chiefly from members of the Richard III Society but also including the local University and other sources. She also negotiated the necessary permissions from the local council, and attracted a TV production company. It was a triumph of facilitation accomplished by independent historians and unpaid volunteers who were often faced with scepticism or indifference. Yet even more fundraising was required from Richard III Society members up to the last minute, without which the remains may still lie under car park tarmac in Leicester, or in a re-filled archaeological trench, and potentially awaiting destruction by future building development. Throughout the book the team's learned approach, historical and scientific understanding, clarity of purpose and years of dedication are fully revealed. We are all in their debt.

The *Looking For Richard Project* team has truly re-written history – so read on and find out exactly how they did it.

Dr Christopher Thornton, FSA, FRHistS
Associate Fellow, Institute of Historical Research
May 2014

1
Death and Burial: *Sine ullo funere honore*

On 22 August 1485 Richard III was killed at the battle of Bosworth (known variously at the time as Redemore[1] or Sandeford[2]). According to the contemporary report of the chronicle of Crowland Abbey, 'he received many mortal wounds and, like a spirited and most courageous prince, fell in battle on the field and not in flight' (*Nam inter pugnandum et non in fuga ... Richardus multis letalibus vulneribus ictus quasi princeps animosus et audentissimus in campo occubuit*).

In death his body was widely reported as subjected to indignities: 'many other insults were offered', the Crowland chronicle remarks, which included having a felon's halter placed around his neck as he was carried to Leicester 'with insufficient humanity' (*multasque alias contumelias illatus ipsoque non satis humaniter propter funem in collum adjectum usque ad Leicestriam deportato*).[3]

On arrival in Leicester Richard's body was exposed to public gaze, as the new King Henry VII announced in a public proclamation: '... brought dede of the feld unto the towne of Leicestre, and ther was laide oppenly that every man mighe se and luke upon him'.[4]

Reliable sources for what happened during the ensuing days in Leicester are scant and inconsistent, but some accounts mention his body being taken to 'the Newarke', which is generally held to refer to the Church of the Annunciation of the Blessed Virgin Mary, known as St Mary-in-the-Newark, a Lancastrian foundation. The Frowyk Chronicle reports that Richard was '... bered atte Laycet[er] in the newe vorke'.[5]

This assertion that he was buried in the Newark has given rise to the tentative suggestion that he might have been interred there, at least initially.[6] However, since his eventual grave is consistently reported to have been in the Franciscan Priory Church at Leicester, a temporary interment followed by exhumation appears to receive little corroboration. The most likely

---

[1] York Civic Records, 23 August 1485: '... [i]t was shewed by div[er]se p[er]sonnes ... send unto the feld of Redemore to bring tiding[es]', [memorandum]: '... apud Rodemore jux[a] Leicestre, fuit bellum'; BL.MS Harl. 541 (*The Frowyk Chronicle, 1482–87*): 'King Richard was scleyne at Redmore feld'.

[2] Proclamation Henry VII addressed to the citizens of York, 25 August 1485: '... was slayne at a place called Sandeford, within the shyre of Leicestre' (*Drake's Eboracum*, p. 121).

[3] *The Crowland Chronicle Continuations 1459–1486*, ed. N. Pronay & J. Cox (1986), pp. 182–3. See also references to Richard III's death in the *Great Chronicle of London*, ed. A.H. Thomas & I.D. Thornley, pp. 237–8; Robert Fabyan, *The Concordaunce of Hystoryes* (1559) Vol. 2, p. 520; Edward Hall, *The Union of the Two Noble and Illustre Famelies of Lancastre and Yorke* (1548), fol. lvii (r & v).

[4] Proclamation Henry VII addressed to the citizens of York, 25 August 1485 (*Drake's Eboracum*, p.121).

[5] BL.MS Harl. 541 (*The Frowyk Chronicle, 1482-87*): '... And bered atte Laycet[er] in the newe vorke'; BL.MS Harl. 542 (*The Ballad of Bosworth Feilde*), fol. 34 and BL Add. MS 27879, fol. 434: '... and in Newark was he laid, that many a man might see.'

[6] A.F. Sutton & L. Visser-Fuchs, 'The Making of a Minor London Chronicle in the Household of Sir Thomas Frowyk (died 1485)', *The Ricardian*, Vol. X, No. 126 (September 1994), pp. 97–8.

explanation for references to 'the Newarke' is that St Mary-in-the-Newark was chosen as the location for the public display of the late king's body on arrival in Leicester.

The Warwickshire priest and antiquary John Rous, writing after 1486 and before 1491, states that 'finally' he was 'buried in the choir of the Friars Minor at Leicester' (*finaliter apud fratres Minores Leicestriæ in choro est sepultus*).[7] In the *Anglica Historia*, commissioned by Richard's successor Henry VII, Polydore Vergil indicates that the new king arrived in Leicester on the evening of 22 August and 'tarried for two days' to make preparations for moving on towards London (*versus parandi causa duos moratur dies*). His version has Richard's body 'conveyed to the convent of Franciscan monks [*sic*] at Leicester … and there buried two days after' (*Ricardi corpus … Lecestriam ad coenobium Franciscanorum monachorum deportatur … biduo post terra humatur*). The first half of this sentence confuses monks with friars, but overall it appears that his burial was effected on the same day as Henry VII's departure, i.e. on 25 August.[8]

Although a variety of fifteenth-century writers came up with their own ideas of his burial place, the reports of Rous and Vergil mentioning the Greyfriars received first-hand confirmation from two sixteenth-century chroniclers, John Leland and Raphael Holinshed, writing within *c*.60-90 years of Richard's death. This and other evidence is discussed below in section 3 ('Memorials of Richard III').

Polydore Vergil, having reported with satisfaction that Richard's body was transported to Leicester 'naked of all clothing' on the back of a horse with his arms and legs hanging on each side (*cuncto nudatum vestitu ac dorso equi impositum, capite et brachiis ac cruribus utrinque pendentibus*), completed the picture of disparagement by noting that his interment was afforded no funeral solemnity (*sine ullo funere honore*).[9] In this he was followed by succeeding writers. The brothers would of necessity have given Richard proper Christian burial in accordance with the rites of the Catholic Church, therefore Vergil's comment should be taken to indicate that no solemn ceremonial took place, such as would have been appropriate to the rank of an anointed king. This omission was germane to the ethos of the retrieval and reburial project.

---

[7] John Rous, *Historia Johannis Rossi Warwicensis de Regibus Anglie*, fol. 136, ed. Thomas Hearne (1716), p. 218. Completed possibly *c*.1490 (attributions to 1486 are almost certainly in error as Rous failed to remember the precise year of Bosworth, the last digit being added later).
[8] Polydore Vergil, *Anglica Historia* (1555), Lib. XXV, The Philological Museum (http://www.philological.bham.ac.uk/polverg/25lat.html).
[9] *Ibid.*

2
Mendicant Orders and the Layout of
a Mediaeval Priory

Following defeat at Bosworth and exposure of his remains to public view in Leicester, Richard III was said by John Rous (pre-1492) and Polydore Vergil (post-1512) to have been buried in the Priory Church of the Franciscan friars (Greyfriars), a Mendicant order whose precinct lay between Leicester Guildhall and St Martin's Church on its northern side, and the town wall to the south. As mentioned above, John Rous specified the burial place as the choir of the Priory Church. Understanding the probable layout of a Franciscan priory was therefore crucial for locating its choir and the possible site of Richard's tomb on the ground.

Mendicant orders are religious orders of the Catholic Church which traditionally depend on charity for their livelihood. They comprise chiefly Franciscans (Greyfriars), Dominicans (Blackfriars), Carmelites (Whitefriars), and Augustinians (Austin friars).[10] Such orders were founded in the late twelfth or early thirteenth centuries and spread through Western Europe in the thirteenth century. The Franciscans were introduced to England in 1224.

Unlike monks, the friars of the Mendicant orders were not confined to their religious house, but worked out in the community. One of their key roles was participation in the public ministry of the Church, and this included preaching to the people.[11] As a result, while their cloisters and the choir of their priory church were normally inaccessible to those who were not members of the religious order, it was essential for the *nave* of their priory church to be accessible to the laity. In the case of religious houses situated in small villages (e.g. Little Walsingham, Norfolk; Clare, Suffolk, see Fig. 1) this presented no problem. For friaries situated in towns it normally meant that the church needed to be located near a public highway, in order that the lay people of the town could have ready access to the nave of the church. The best preserved example of what this meant in terms of the location of the church building can very clearly be seen in Norwich, where the former Dominican Priory survives as a concert hall and meeting rooms.

The Dominican Priory in Norwich also raises another very important issue. Like all mediaeval churches, priory churches were always orientated west-east, with the choir at the

---

[10] Other, less well-known Mendicant orders include Servites, Trinitarians, Minims and Mercedarians.

[11] 'In 1224 Francis decided to send some friars to England and appointed Agnellus of Pisa to lead a small expedition. …Within seven weeks of arrival they had established friaries in Canterbury, London and Oxford, the ecclesiastical, political and intellectual capitals of England. The friars served the poor and the outcast and preached the Gospel to them' http://www.friar.org/about-us/our-heritage.html (April 2014); 'Francis of Assisi referred to himself as the 'Herald of the Great King', someone called to tell others of the love of God in Jesus Christ. He was a gifted preacher who summoned people to repentance, a turning around of their lives; and to live in harmony with God's abundant generosity and compassion. Franciscan brothers and sisters today are often involved in sharing the Good News – through preaching' http://www.franciscans.org.uk/living-as-franciscans/sharing-the-gospel (April 2014); 'The Franciscans proved enormously popular because, like Francis himself, they fulfilled a desperate need, in fact a whole series of them. … The mendicants settled in the cities and developed a program of preaching and pastoral guidance' http://www.fordham.edu/halsall/source/stfran-rule.html (April 2014).

eastern end and the nave at the western end. In the case of the Norwich Dominican Priory the church was aligned adjacent to a road which also ran east-west, and which lay on the southern side of the church. Thus the cloisters (through which lay people were not allowed to pass) had to be sited on the north side of the church.

However, another Norwich mendicant priory had a different orientation. The Norwich Carmelite Priory Church was noted by Dr John Ashdown-Hill to be aligned with its western end adjoining a roadway. Thus the Carmelite Priory could have had its cloisters situated either on the north side of the church, or on the south side. Ashdown-Hill predicted that the cloisters lay on the south side. Other researchers suggested that the cloisters were sited to the north of the church. In the case of the Norwich Carmel this issue has not yet been resolved.

A similar situation existed in mediaeval Leicester. There, for example, the Augustinian Priory (Austin Friars) was located outside the town walls (i.e. in a semi-rural area) and, like the Norwich Carmel, its church was orientated with the western end of the nave fronting a roadway. As a result, access to the Austin Friars Church would have been completely unaffected by the positioning of the cloisters.[12] In theory, the friars would have been free to place their cloisters either on the north of their church or on the south, as in the case of the Norwich Carmel. In actual fact, excavation has shown that they built their church towards the southern end of the site, with their cloisters to the north of the church.

On the other hand Leicester's Franciscan Priory had an entirely different location, with a significant highway on its *northern* side. As a result, the Franciscan friars would have been absolutely obliged to take account of access for lay visitors when deciding the relative locations of their church and cloisters. The only realistic option open to them was to build the church on the northern side of the site, adjacent to the road, and then place the cloisters (inaccessible to the laity) on the southern side of the church.

While the cloister and domestic buildings might be situated either on the north side of the church or on the south side (depending on the location of the site), typically the friaries and churches of mediaeval Mendicant religious houses did follow a standard plan (see Figs 1 & 5). The nave, at the western end of the church, often had side aisles, but the choir, at the eastern end, normally had none, and usually the church had no transepts (i.e. was not cruciform in plan). The nave and choir were normally separated by an *ambulacrum*, 'slype' or walkway which gave access from the street through to the domestic buildings of the priory. Above the slype there was normally a bell tower (often octagonal in plan), surmounted by a spire (Fig.3).[13]

During the period approximately 1995-2010, in connection with his wider historical research, Ashdown-Hill studied a number of Mendicant religious houses, including Walsingham Greyfriars,[14] Norwich Blackfriars, Colchester Greyfriars, Norwich Whitefriars,[15] Clare Priory (Austin friars),[16] and Leicester Greyfriars. The evidence from well-preserved buildings or ruins, such as Walsingham Greyfriars and the Norwich Blackfriars, and also of well excavated sites such as Clare, helped inform his predictions of the likely layout of less well-preserved and less well-researched sites, such as the Colchester Greyfriars, the Norwich Whitefriars, and the Leicester Greyfriars. Illustrated below are plans of well-documented priories, together with his tentative plans and elevations for the less well-documented examples.

---

[12] Compare, for example, Norwich Carmelite Priory. Like the Leicester Austin Friars, this is another priory where the west end of the church fronted on to a road. Ashdown-Hill suggests that the cloisters lay to the south of the church – though others have suggested that the cloisters perhaps lay to the north.

[13] A. Martin, *Franciscan Architecture in England*, British Society for Franciscan Studies 18 (1937).

[14] Patronised by Richard III's ancestors.

[15] The burial site of Eleanor Talbot, alleged first wife of Edward IV.

[16] The burial site of members of Richard III's ancestral family, including Lionel of Antwerp, Duke of Clarence, and Edmund Mortimer, Earl of March.

The total research cited in this section comprises the basic evidence for location of the burial site of Richard III used by Philippa Langley, John Ashdown-Hill and the Looking For Richard Project from 2005 to 2012.

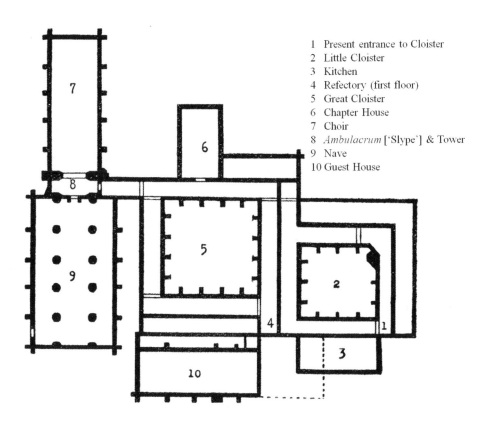

1   Present entrance to Cloister
2   Little Cloister
3   Kitchen
4   Refectory (first floor)
5   Great Cloister
6   Chapter House
7   Choir
8   *Ambulacrum* ['Slype'] & Tower
9   Nave
10 Guest House

Fig. 1: A typical Mendicant Priory plan: Walsingham Greyfriars.
Published in Fr Gilbert, OFMCap, PhD, What to see in Walsingham (1948), p. 69.
In this case the cloisters are on the south of the church.

*Fig. 2: Site of the Leicester Franciscan Priory Church –
as predicted by Ashdown-Hill in 2005*

*Fig. 3: Elevation of the Leicester Franciscan Priory Church
looking south from St Martin's – as predicted by Ashdown-Hill in*
The Last Days of Richard III *in 2010, plate 23.*

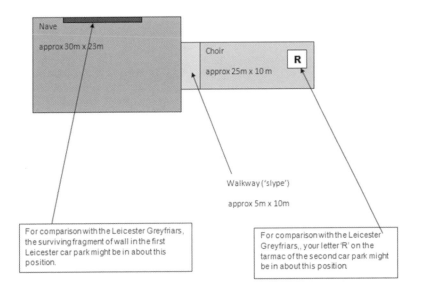

Rough dimensions of the surviving

Norwich Blackfriars former church

Fig. 4: Plan of the Norwich Dominican Priory Church, predicting how this might relate to the size, position and layout of the Leicester Franciscan Priory Church. This sketch was drawn from memory by Ashdown-Hill whilst employed at Zirve University, Turkey and was sent to Philippa Langley by email on 10 February 2012 and used by her at the dig. The general plan and north-south location of the Leicester Franciscan Priory Church, as indicated here, were correctly predicted, but when excavated in August-September 2012 the church was found to lie a little farther to the east.

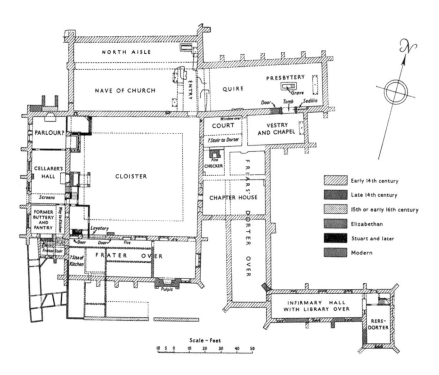

Fig. 5: Clare Priory, a priory church whose nave had only a north aisle.
Published in K.W. Barnardiston, Clare Priory *(1962), p. 2.*

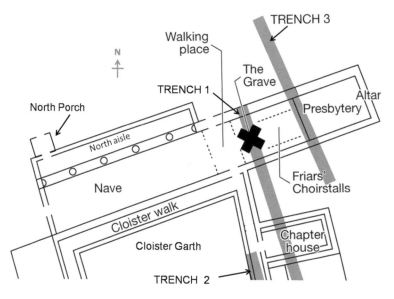

Fig. 6: Leicester Franciscan Priory Church – Ashdown-Hill's predicted plan
showing only a north aisle, as at Clare Priory, published in 2nd (2013) edition of
The Last Days of Richard III, *plate 41.*

The founder of the Franciscan Priory in Leicester is unknown, although local tradition ascribes responsibility to Simon de Montfort, Earl of Leicester. The layout of the priory precinct was long debated, and comprised one of the crucial factors in attempting to predict the likely site of Richard III's grave. The Franciscan Priory occupied a large walled precinct to the south of a principal mediaeval thoroughfare connecting Leicester's High Street and the South Gate with the Saturday market to the east. A small surviving stretch of mediaeval wall adjacent to this road comprises the only surviving visible evidence of the mediaeval priory above ground level.

Having their priory church located adjacent to such a thoroughfare was very important to the friars, since it permitted ready access to the nave of the priory church for those lay people who wished to hear the friars preaching. As has already been noted above, Ashdown-Hill therefore predicted that the friars would probably have constructed their priory church on the northern side of their precinct, as proved the case (see above, Figs 2, 4 & 6).

Other opinions prevailed in Leicester. An article by David Baldwin, published in 1986, suggested that Richard III's burial place lay at the extreme eastern end of the Greyfriars site, under the modern Grey Friars street, or under one of the neighbouring buildings.[17] Following Baldwin's publication, in 1990 the Richard III Society erected a memorial to Richard III on a former bank on the eastern side of this street.

More recently, a reconstruction of the Franciscan Priory layout published by archaeological contractors ULAS in 2011 proposed that the church had been sited on the southern side of the Greyfriars precinct, close to the town wall (see Fig. 7).[18] Ashdown-Hill considered the layout proposed by ULAS unlikely, since it would have made it difficult for lay people to access the nave of the priory church without passing through the cloister area which would not have been permitted. In addition, the published ULAS reconstruction did not conform to the normal appearance of a mediaeval friars' church (see above), with nave, slype and choir.

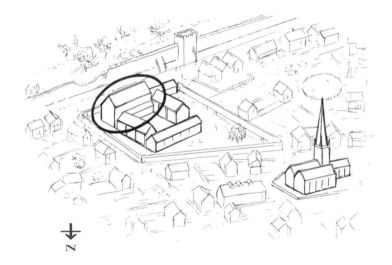

N

Fig. 7: Reconstruction of the mediaeval Franciscan Priory at Leicester by ULAS (University of Leicester Archaeological Services), 2011. Their suggested (incorrect) location of the church has been circled. © Geoffrey Wheeler, redrawn after Mike Codd.

---

[17] D. Baldwin, 'King Richard's Grave in Leicester, *Transactions of Leicestershire Archaeological and Historical Society*, vol. 60, 1986, pp. 21–4 [p. 24].
[18] M. Morris, R. Buckley & M. Codd, *Visions of Ancient Leicester* (2011) p. 46.

That the choir was indeed the location of Richard III's grave within the Franciscan Priory Church was confirmed by records of the tomb which was later constructed to commemorate his resting place (see section 3, 'Memorials of Richard III').

To be buried in the choir of the church, as recorded by Rous, would have been a signal honour reserved for only the most high-status occupants. Despite the haste of Richard III's interment it was entirely appropriate, from every point of view, that he should be laid to rest in this holy area. For Henry VII the advantage of this burial site was that the choir of the priory church would not have been accessible to the general public. The location chosen for Richard III's burial followed the established pattern for the burial of an ousted king.[19]

Nine or ten years after Richard III's death, King Henry VII commissioned a royal tomb of alabaster to be erected over Richard's grave site. As far as can be ascertained, his grave and the later royal tomb then remained undisturbed until Henry VIII's 'Dissolution of the Monasteries', when the Greyfriars foundation was dismantled and would have presented a useful source of reclaimed materials for local townspeople.

The normal pattern during the Dissolution was that the churches of religious houses were reduced to the state of roofless ruins by the king's agents before the precinct was secularized. Typically the lead from the roof was melted down. Then, together with any roof timbers of the church, the lead was sold off by the commissioners before the estate was handed over to its new owners. In the case of the Franciscan Priory Church in Leicester this was presumably done in 1538. The site itself was then sold.

The reduction of the Leicester Franciscan Priory Church to a roofless ruin would have had a damaging effect on Richard III's royal tomb, because alabaster is a soft stone which does not cope well with exposure to the weather. However, despite later reports that Richard III's tomb was destroyed there is no contemporary evidence to show that it was deliberately damaged in any way. The probability is that the tomb simply deteriorated slowly due to rain and frost.

Records show that building material from the priory site was subsequently being sold off until at least 1561.[20] Towards the end of the sixteenth century the former Greyfriars precinct was purchased by Robert Herrick, Mayor of Leicester, whose son (also Robert Herrick, also one-time Mayor) succeeded him. Their house occupied a location to the east of the precinct, probably in the position formerly occupied by the residence of the Guardian (religious head) of the Franciscan Priory. Eventually part of the site was sold in the nineteenth century to the Alderman Newton's Boys' School who built a Victorian schoolhouse, also on the precinct's east side, which on the cessation of Alderman Newton's in the 1980s was occupied by Leicester Grammar School. A wall separated this from the remainder of the site which was purchased by the Leicester Corporation, eventually being acquired by Leicester City Council in 1968 for use as offices. The areas which had not been built upon were reserved as private parking for council staff.

---

[19] J. Ashdown-Hill, *The Last Days of Richard III* (2013), p. 91.

[20] J. Nichols, *The History and Antiquities of the County of Leicester*, Vol. 1, part II (1815), p. 294.

3
Memorials of Richard III

The Greyfriars Tomb

The reign of Henry VII was not universally welcomed. Peppered with disaffection and unrest, especially during the remaining years of the fifteenth century, it had to contend with Yorkist pretenders and uprisings which escalated at times to full-scale battles. In 1494 or 1495, perhaps in an attempt to mollify Yorkist sentiment, Henry VII commissioned a tomb for his predecessor to be set up in the Church of the Leicester Franciscan Priory.

Two sixteenth-century sources confirmed personal knowledge of Richard's interment in the church: John Leland, who visited Leicester before 1543, wrote in his *Itinerary*: 'The Grey-Freres of Leicester stode at the ende of the hospital of Mr Wigeston ... and there was byried King Richard 3 ... These thinges brevely I markid at Leyrcester.'[21] It is possible that the place occupied by Richard's tomb, erected in the 1490s, was still visible when Leland made his visit. Raphael Holinshed also mentioned the tomb, saying that it incorporated 'a picture of alabaster representing [Richard's] person', a description he might have gained from speaking to someone who saw it.[22]

Sir George Buck described the tomb in *The History of King Richard the Third* (1619): 'a fair tomb of mingled colour marble adorned with his image'. Buck also reproduced a copy of his epitaph, which he found 'in a recorded manuscript book, chained to a table in a chamber in the Guildhall of London'.[23] This is just one of a number of surviving transcriptions which are summarized and compared in Appendix 2 below.

Today several details of the commissioning of the tomb are known from contemporaneous documents; one of the earliest citations appears in Caroline Halsted's 1844 biography of Richard III, a landmark work based on painstaking research, in which she quotes Bentley's *Excerpta Historica* (1833), p. 105, and Nichols's *Leicester* (1815): 'Extract from the privy purse expences of King Henry VII, September 11th, an. 1495:- "To James Keyley, for King Richard's tomb, 10*l* 1*s*."'[24]

But the trail of documentation for Richard III's royal tomb starts earlier, with Henry VII's delegation of this project to Sir Reynold Bray and Sir Thomas Lovell, who commissioned a Nottingham alabaster man, Walter Hylton, to erect a monument 'in the Church of Friers in the

---

[21] *The Itinerary of John Leland in or about the years 1535–1543*, ed. L. Toulmin Smith (1907), Vol. 1 p. 15, cited by P.W. Hammond, 'The Burial Place of Richard III', *The Ricardian*, Vol. IV, No. 59 (December 1977), pp. 30–1.
[22] *Holinshed's Chronicles of England, Scotland and Ireland*, Vol. 3 (1808), p. 447 (originally published 1577).
[23] *The History of King Richard the Third by Sir George Buck, Master of the Revels,* ed. A.N. Kincaid (1979), Lib. V, p. 217.
[24] C.A. Halsted, *Richard III as Duke of Gloucester and King of England* (1844), pp. 474–5 and fn. 4.

town of leycestr where the bonys of Kyng Richard the iij^{de} reste'.[25] This was probably that same Walter Hylton who served as Mayor of Nottingham in 1489/90 and again in 1496/97.[26]

We are aware of the commission to Hylton only because it subsequently gave rise to a legal dispute.[27] Following Hylton's commission, an alabaster tomb monument for Richard III was made in Nottingham and subsequently installed at the Franciscan Priory Church in Leicester. The sum paid to Hylton for his work on Richard's tomb is usually reported to have been £50, though in fact the reading of this figure is problematic.[28]

This sum did not represent Henry VII's total expenditure on Richard's tomb. On 11 September 1495, the further payment noted above was made from the privy purse 'to James Keyley for King Rich. Tombe – £10. 0s. 12d.'.[29] It is not stated precisely what exactly Keyley did in respect of the tomb, but one possible clue is provided by another entry dated 20 January [1501?] recording the payment of £10 to Master Estfield 'for conveying of the King's [Henry VII's] Toumbe from Windesor to Westmr'. In a similar way Richard III's tomb may have been made in Nottingham in Walter Hylton's workshop, and then transported to (and set up in?) Leicester by James Keyley. Assuming that the money paid to Keyley was not part of the sum of ?£50 mentioned in connection with Walter Hylton's indenture, but was additional to it, this would bring the total cost of the tomb to not less than (perhaps) £60. It may well have been higher, since the records mentioning Hylton and Keyley survived purely by chance.[30]

No detailed description of Richard III's tomb exists, but it was made by workers in alabaster.[31] As reported by Holinshed (above), alabaster was certainly the material in which the effigy or image of Richard which surmounted the tomb was crafted.[32]

---

[25] TNA:PRO C1/206/69. See note 36 below.

[26] He witnessed a deed on 10 August 1490: Nottinghamshire Archives, DD/P/CD/13. See also http://en.wikipedia.org/wiki/Lord_Mayor_of_Nottingham (consulted June 2009).

[27] The plea is dated on the reverse 1 July 11 Henry VII [1496].

[28] R. Edwards, 'King Richard's Tomb in Leicester', *The Ricardian* Vol. III No. 50 (September 1975), pp. 8-9, citing TNA:PRO C1/206/69. This is a record of a chancery case brought by Rauf Hill of Nottingham against Walter Hylton, alleging the fraudulent insertion of Rauf's name in indentures between Hylton and Sir Reynold Bray and Sir Thomas Lovell concerning the making of a tomb for Richard III. About one third of this manuscript is now virtually unreadable. The supposed figure of £50 for the cost of the tomb is an interpretation advanced by a previous researcher – who may indeed have been able to decipher more of the text than is now legible. John Ashdown-Hill's examination of the manuscript did not succeed in substantiating this figure, though two separate references to 'xv li' and 'xx li' respectively were found.

[29] The payment to James Keyley mentions no year. Nevertheless, the precise date can be ascertained because the preceding folio records the payment of £10 to Sir William Stanley 'at his execution'. This entry is dated 20 February, and Stanley was executed in February 1495. Thus the payment to Keyley was clearly made on 11 September 1495.

[30] For purposes of comparison, in the 1450s an alabaster retable for an altar (roughly the equivalent in size of one side of a table tomb) cost £1 17s. 3d., while in 1462 an alabaster image of the Virgin Mary (size unspecified) could be purchased for £2: J. Blair and N. Ramsey, eds., *English Medieval Industries* (1991), p. 37. A surviving contract, drawn up in 1508, for a fine alabaster table tomb for Henry Foljambe of Chesterfield, Derbyshire specifies a cost of £10 for the tomb table, decorated with small effigies and shields bearing arms on the side panels. In this case the table was to be topped off with gilt copper effigies which are presumed not to have been included in the price of £10: Blair and Ramsey, *English Medieval Industries*, p. 35; J.C. Cox, *Memorials of Old Derbyshire* (1907), p. 108. The only recorded expenditure for the original tomb of Cecily Neville, Richard III's mother, was 100 marks (roughly £66).[30]

[31] Although Richard's epitaph describes its stone as 'marble', this was a very common late mediaeval synonym for alabaster.

[32] Whether Richard's alabaster 'picture' actually comprised a statue or a flat engraved slab is uncertain. Alabaster tomb effigies were very common at this period, and were almost mass-produced. Surviving incised alabaster slabs from the end of the fifteenth century are rarer – though not unknown. The tomb of

Henry VII's provision of £10 1s for the tomb was established fact long before the twentieth century, but little further research on it seems to have been done until 1975 when Rhoda Edwards (author of the indispensable *Itinerary of Richard III*)[33] was the first to discover the important contents of TNA:PRO document C1/206/69 which records the Chancery proceedings of Rauf Hill against Walter Hylton.[34] She reported that Hylton's payment was to be in two instalments: £20 initially, and the residue when the 'Tombe were set up and fynysshed in the Church aforeseid'. That church was 'named first in error as the "Newark" which was then crossed out and "of Friers" substituted'.

It should perhaps be mentioned that although in retrospect we can say with confidence that Richard III's eventual grave and tomb were situated in the Leicester Franciscan Priory Church, this is in fact far from being the only location mentioned in surviving fifteenth-century accounts.

The two earliest accounts say Richard III was buried:

- in a 'little hermitage' (Diego de Valera, 1486)
- at the Newark in Leicester (Frowyk Chronicle, 1485)

Documents written shortly afterwards say Richard was buried:

- 'in the choir of the Friars Minor' (John Rous *c*.1490 supported by Polydore Vergil *c*.1513)
- 'in a dike like a dogge' (William Burton, York Records, 1491)
- in 'a village church' (Jean Molinet, *c*.1500)

The Greyfriars has generally been favoured over other locations, partly because it is mentioned by Rous and Vergil, two credible early sources (whereas no corroboration exists for the other sites), and partly because of apparently reliable records of a later memorial erected at the Franciscan Priory Church. Nevertheless, the Frowyk Chronicle contained a report from a participant at the battle of Bosworth which said that Richard was buried at the Newark (see page 7 above); a point that was examined by Anne Sutton and Livia Visser-Fuchs in *The Ricardian* in 1994.[35] They felt it was possible that Richard's body might not only have been exhibited there, but also buried there, if only temporarily. In this context John Ashdown-Hill sought further evidence to clarify the position, and in the course of researches for his book, *The Last Days of Richard III*, had occasion to revisit TNA:PRO C1/206/69. One clear sentence stood out, not given in full by Edwards or by Baldwin. Edwards had ascertained that 'Newark' was deleted in favour of the word 'Friers', but lines 4-5 (on folio 69 recto) in their entirety left no doubt about the precise location of the tomb and the bones it was destined to commemorate: 'in the Church of Friers in the town of leycestr where the bonys of Kyng Richard the iii[de] reste'.[36] This appeared to establish beyond doubt that, by 1494 at the latest, Richard III's remains were buried in a friary church in Leicester; and the only friary church ever mentioned in connection with Richard's burial was the Greyfriars.

William Shore, erstwhile husband of Edward IV's last mistress, is marked by an incised alabaster effigy, similar in appearance to a 'brass'. See J. Ashdown-Hill, *Richard III's Beloved Cousyn* (2009), figure 19.
[33] R. Edwards, *The Itinerary of King Richard III 1483-1485* (1983, 1995).
[34] R. Edwards, 'King Richard's Tomb in Leicester', *The Ricardian* Vol. III No. 50 (September 1975), pp. 8-9.
[35] A.F. Sutton & L. Visser-Fuchs, 'The Making of a Minor London Chronicle in the Household of Sir Thomas Frowyk (died 1485)', *The Ricardian*, Vol. X No. 126 (September 1994), pp. 86-103 (pp. 97-98).
[36] TNA:PRO C1/206/69 recto, lines 4 and 5, published in J. Ashdown-Hill, *The Last Days of Richard III* (2010) p. 97.

Robert Herrick's Pillar

There is no reason to believe that Richard III's tomb was deliberately destroyed at the Dissolution (see above). In general, records show that tombs remained standing in ruined monastic and conventual churches until at least the end of the sixteenth century.[37] Richard's royal tomb must have been well remembered in the church ruins when the Herrick family first purchased the Greyfriars site.

Certainly, it was anything but forgotten. Alderman Robert Herrick, a one-time Mayor of Leicester, whose father of the same name had purchased the site on which he built a splendid house, proudly displayed in his garden a three-foot pillar commemorating the former king's burial site. This was recorded in 1612 by Christopher Wren, B.D., the future Dean of Windsor, and father of the architect of St Paul's Cathedral, who was tutor to Robert Herrick's nephew at St John's College, Oxford. Dr Wren wrote the following in a letter, later published by his son:[38] 'the place of his burial ... being after purchased by Mr Robert Heyrick, some time mayor of Leicester, was by him covered by a handsome stone pillar three feet high, with this inscription, "Here lies the body of Richard III., some time King of England." This he shewed me walking in his garden, 1612.'[39]

What subsequently became of this 'handsome stone pillar' is unknown. One possibility is that 'it may not have survived the taking of Leicester by the Royalists [during the English Civil War], when desperate fighting took place near St Martin's Church [Cathedral] which was immediately north of the Grey Friars' grounds'.[40]

Myths and Traditions

Despite this fine commemoration of Richard III's last resting place, a curious story began to be circulated in Leicester at precisely the time (1612) that Wren saw the Herrick family's memorial in their garden. This story told of how a jeering mob disinterred Richard's remains at the time of the Dissolution and carried them through the streets of Leicester, eventually disposing of them at Bow Bridge. As John Speede first reported this story, more than three-quarters of a century after the Dissolution, 'his Tombe ... at the suppression of that Monastery [*sic*] was pulled downe, and utterly defaced; since when his grave overgrown with nettles and weedes, is very obscure and not to be found. Only the stone chest wherin his corpse lay is now made a drinking trough for horses at a common Inne, and retaineth the onely memory of this Monarches greatnesse. His body also (as tradition hath delivered) was borne out of the City and contemptuously bestowed under the end of *Bow-Bridge*'.[41] It is noteworthy that Speede suggests the body was reburied, not that it was thrown into the river, as later versions of the tale suggested.

This was subsequently developed to produce the myth of Richard III having been hurled into the river, first related by John Throsby in the late eighteenth century: 'his bones taken in triumph thro' the streets; and at last thrown, over the bridge over which he rode to the fatal

---

[37] Elizabeth I's agents found the tombs of her Yorkist royal ancestors still intact in the ruined east end of Fotheringhay Church in the 1590s, when the queen ordered the remains to be reburied in the surviving western end of the church. John Weever later found and recorded many surviving tombs in dissolved religious house ruins in the early years of the seventeenth century: J. Weever, *Ancient Funeral Monuments* (1631).

[38] C. Wren, *Parentalia, or Memoirs of the Family of the Wrens*, (1750) p.144.

[39] C.A. Halsted, *Richard III*, Vol. II, p. 478.

[40] Richard III Society, Barton Library, personal communication from S.H. Skillington, Hon. Secretary, Leicester Archaeological Society, to Saxon Barton, 29 October 1935.

[41] J. Speede [Speed], *The History of Great Britaine* (1611, 1614), p. 725.

battle of Bosworth'; no source is offered for the story.[42] These tales were scarcely challenged during the centuries that followed; although Caroline Halsted (1844), who accepted that his tomb might have been defaced and his remains disturbed, doubted that they were actually removed from the grave. Its whereabouts, she felt, were no longer known. Paul Murray Kendall (1955) made no reference to the disposal of Richard's remains, but the myth was deeply embedded locally, as was the tale of the (anachronistic) stone coffin used as a drinking-trough, an object of which no trace existed after the mid 1740s, although its memory lingered on. In Charles Ross's biography of Richard III (1981), at one time considered the standard work, Professor Ross surprisingly reported that 'the Franciscan convent was dissolved, the bones were thrown out and the coffin became a horse-trough outside the White Horse Inn'.[43]

In 2004 the BBC commissioned Ashdown-Hill to write an article for their *Local Legends* website on the story that Richard III's remains were dug up at the Dissolution and thrown into the river Soar. On the basis of the evidence of Herrick's pillar, he concluded that the story was unlikely. He had earlier researched the commemorative plaque erected on a building adjacent to Bow Bridge in 1856 by a Leicester resident, Mr Benjamin Broadbent, which read 'Near this spot lie the remains of Richard III, the last of the Plantagenets, 1485'. According to correspondence in the Barton Library of the Richard III Society, Ashdown-Hill found that Broadbent himself had admitted his plaque relied purely on local tradition. A letter dated 1935 from the Hon. Secretary of the Leicestershire Archaeological Society stated 'There is no reason whatever to attach any value to it'. Another letter, from the Keeper of Antiquities at the City of Leicester Museums and Art Gallery (1955), did not think there could be much doubt either of the place of Richard's burial or of 'the groundlessness of the desecration story'.

Accordingly, at Ashdown-Hill's prompting, the Richard III Society donated an explanatory plaque to the City of Leicester which was erected in 2005 near the earlier one at Bow Bridge, stating that the tradition was 'now generally discredited'. This in no way deterred a succession of writers and historians from continuing to repeat the tradition of the bones being disinterred as if it were fact. The tenacity of Speede's story was such that it was actually repeated by the archaeologists in 2012 *in the official application for a licence* to exhume those remains at the Greyfriars which proved to be Richard III (see Appendix 6 below).

Ashdown-Hill's ongoing work on the subject, subsequently published in *The Last Days of Richard III* [44] revealed two points which seemed to have escaped previous attention. First, the 'bones in the river' story was not the account recorded by Speede in 1611. As has already been noted (above), Speede's account said rather that Richard III had been dug up and then *reburied* under Bow Bridge. Even more interesting was the context for Speede's story. He explained that he had visited the priory site and looked for evidence of the grave, but had found no sign of it – only weeds and nettles. Thus it was in the context of his failure to find any trace of Richard III's grave that Speede apparently invented the story of the king's removal and reburial. On examining the map of Leicester drawn by Speede, Ashdown-Hill saw that the location marked as 'Grey Friars' was an error. It was actually the site of the Blackfriars (Dominican) Priory. The real Greyfriars site was not indicated at all.[45] The obvious conclusion was that Speede had searched for traces of Richard's grave – and had found only weeds and nettles – in the wrong

---

[42] John Throsby, *History and Antiquities of the Ancient Town of Leicester* (1791), p. 64; C.J. Billson, *Mediaeval Leicester* (1920), p. 186, noted that this embellishment first appeared in Throsby.

[43] P.M. Kendall, *Richard III* (1955); C. Ross, *Richard III* (1981), p. 226.

[44] J. Ashdown-Hill, *The Last Days of Richard III* (2010), p. 134; (2013), p. 157.

[45] The mistake on Speede's map had been noted by John Throsby (*op. cit.*) and by John Nichols, *The History and Antiquities of the County of Leicester* (1795-1811), but neither connected this with the fact that Speede was unable to find any trace of Richard III's tomb when seeking it on what he thought was the Greyfriars site; nor with the fact that Speede then put forward the story that the king's remains had been disinterred at the Reformation.

place. No previous publication made this crucial connection between Speede's erroneous marking of the Greyfriars site and his invented story that Richard III's body had been moved.[46]

There is no other known record of vindictive desecration of graves at the time of Henry VIII's 'Dissolution of the Monasteries',[47] and Leicester had no particular quarrel with Richard III which might account for such behaviour. However, the ingenious suggestion has been made that the story might have been linked to a previous occurrence. Audrey Strange, writing on the subject in 1975, made the connection: 'The bones of John Wycliffe a few miles away at Lutterworth actually were disinterred, burned and thrown into the river in 1425.'[48] Since there seems no other reason for John Speede to have written down his improbable tale of the 'jeering mob', perhaps he, or his Leicester informant, had been told of the Wycliffe incident and misremembered it.

Mendicant and Monastic Orders – Some Notable Burials and Reburials
(burials at mendicant churches are marked with *)

Name	First burial	Reburial(s)
Joan, daughter of Edward I	*Clare Priory, 1307	-
Margaret, Queen to Edward I	*Franciscan Priory, Newgate, 1318	-
Isabelle, Queen to Edward II	*Franciscan Priory, Newgate, 1358	-
Lionel, Duke of Clarence	*Clare Priory, 1358	-
King Richard II	*Dominican Priory, King's Langley, 1399/1400	Westminster Abbey, 1413
Edmund Mortimer, 5th Earl of March	*Clare Priory, 1425	-
Richard, Duke of York	Pontefract Priory, 1460	Fotheringhay Collegiate Church, 1476
Edmund, Earl of Rutland	Pontefract Priory, 1460	Fotheringhay Collegiate Church, 1476
King Henry VI	Chertsey Abbey, 1471	St George's Chapel, Windsor, 1484
Anne Mowbray, Duchess of York	Westminster Abbey, 1481	1) *Abbey of the Minoresses, Aldgate, 1502 2) Westminster Abbey, 1965
John Howard, Duke of Norfolk	Leicester (place unknown), 1485	1) Thetford Priory, c.1489 2) Framlingham Church, c.1554

---

[46] J. Ashdown-Hill, *The Last Days of Richard III* (2010), pp. 105-08; (2013), pp. 106-09; and plate 28.

[47] It is important to emphasize the distinction between tombs and *shrines*. Shrines were destroyed, and the bones they contained were usually reinterred in unmarked graves, to prevent further pilgrimages. In the case of Thomas Becket it is even reported that his bones were destroyed: J. Butler, *The Quest for Becket's Bones* (London, 1995), pp. 32-3, 161-5.

[48] A. Strange, 'The Grey Friars, Leicester', *The Ricardian*, Vol. III No. 50 (September 1975), pp. 3-7.

4
Modern Research

The Richard III Society, although managed on a voluntary basis and open to all comers, lacks no academic rigour. Its journal, *The Ricardian*, has long been a forum for specialist articles on subjects relating to the fifteenth century from contributors who regularly include most of the leading mediaeval historians of the day. To those who have but a superficial interest in late mediaeval England, the Society's work may be unfamiliar. It has nonetheless made an immense contribution to the knowledge of the period, offering members several libraries and librarians, research committees, a publications arm which has undertaken projects of outstanding historical significance, together with exponents of palaeography and several mediaeval languages including Latin.

The final resting place of Richard III's body has been a subject of interest since the Society's inception, and in 1975-78 a number of articles in *The Ricardian* discussed this topic and speculated as to where in modern Leicester the site of the Franciscan Priory Church might be located. The first such article, contributed by Leicester resident Audrey Strange, examined the nature and history of the Franciscan friars, the layout of their priories, and why their church was a natural choice of burial place for the late king.[49] Taken for the most part from secondary sources, her article included an interesting little sketch-plan of Leicester in which she very accurately depicted the Franciscan Priory Church on the northern side of the priory precinct, opposite St Martin's Church (now Leicester Cathedral) and between the present (post-mediaeval) streets known as New Street and Grey Friars; she also indicated the location of the Newarke where Richard's body was exhibited to the public (see Fig. 8).

Her article mentioned the known fact that Henry VII had 'arranged for a tomb with King Richard's likeness' to be erected on his grave at the Greyfriars, and referred to Alderman Robert Herrick's commemorative pillar. Incidentally, her article gave no source for her information about the pillar: possibly an indication of her view that this and its source were already well known and generally accepted. It had, after all, been cited by Halsted. And having derived various other traditional local stories from C.J. Billson's *Mediaeval Leicester* (1920), in which the account of the pillar had also appeared, this might simply have been an oversight in footnoting.

Discussing the tradition that Richard's bones had been thrown into the river Soar, it was Audrey Strange who made the connection with the desecration of the bones of John Wycliffe (mentioned above in section 3 'Memorials of Richard III'). Clearly Strange viewed the river Soar story with disbelief, for she ended by stating her opinion that King Richard's remains still resided at the Greyfriars under one of the council parking areas. *This appears to have been the first statement to this effect ever published.*

In the same issue as the foregoing was the article by Rhoda Edwards mentioned already,[50] in which she was the first to reveal the record of the plea by Rauf Hill against Walter Hylton in

---

[49] A. Strange, 'The Grey Friars, Leicester', *The Ricardian* Vol. III No. 50 (September 1975), pp. 3-7.
[50] R. Edwards, 'King Richard's Tomb in Leicester', *The Ricardian* Vol. III No. 50 (September 1975), pp. 8-9.

TNA:PRO C1/206/69. In 1977 the Society's research officer, Peter W. Hammond, wrote a brief summary about Richard's burial place,[51] confirming that it was usually said to have been in the 'Grey Friars' Church in Leicester (i.e. the Franciscan Priory Church): 'since not long after his death this has been given as the site of his tomb, and there appears no reason to doubt it.' Noting that this had been disputed, Hammond assembled confirmatory accounts recorded by John Rous, Polydore Vergil, the Rauf Hill/Walter Hylton case, and the *Itinerary* of John Leland. He pointed out that in the report of Chancery proceedings against Hylton the tomb was specifically placed in the church 'of Friers'. The document had initially named the church as the Newark, 'but this was deleted, a change which would not have been made if there had been any doubt that the tomb was in a Friary'.

MEDIEVAL LEICESTER

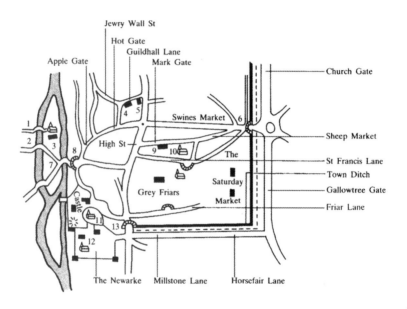

KEY
1. Little Bow Bridge
2. Bow Bridge
3. The Austin Friars
4. Old Mayor's Hall
5. Blue Boar Inn
6. East Gate
7. West Bridge
8. West Gate
9. Guildhall
10. St. Martin's Church now the Cathedral
11. St. Mary-de-Castro
12. St. Mary in the Newarke
13. South Gate

Fig. 8: Plan of the mediaeval Greyfriars precinct and environs by Audrey Strange, 1975

---

[51] P.W. Hammond, 'The Burial Place of Richard III', *The Ricardian* Vol. IV No. 59 (December 1977), pp. 30-1.

The following year the Museum of London's distinguished osteoarchaeologist Dr William J. White contributed an article to *The Ricardian* about mediaeval burial practice.[52] After discussing the unsubstantiated 'bones in the river' story, he stated his opinion 'there is reason to believe that [Richard III's] body was undisturbed and is located in that part of the Greyfriars site now underlying a car park'.

In 1986 the Leicester-based historian David Baldwin published 'King Richard's Grave in Leicester',[53] an article which has recently been claimed by the University of Leicester as the key source for all the information leading to the excavation of the Greyfriars site in 2012. It therefore needs to be considered carefully.

Baldwin cites TNA:PRO C1/206/69. However, he does so via the *Ricardian* article by Rhoda Edwards cited above.[54] His text reads 'Hylton was to receive £50 [*sic*] for the work payable in two instalments, £20 initially, and the balance when the "Tombe were set up and fynysshed in the Church (of Friers) aforesaid"'.[55] This quotation is derived directly from Edwards's text – though omitting her stated reservations about the total cost, given that she had found the sum 'almost unreadable'. There is therefore no indication as to whether or not David Baldwin himself consulted the original very faded manuscript at the Public Record Office (now The National Archives). He offers no new material from its text. Thus, in 1986, the key published author in respect of this particular topic was Edwards rather than Baldwin.

Baldwin did not cite Audrey Strange's article; however, he reiterated her report of the Herrick pillar, together with mention of the earliest account of the story that the king's remains were disinterred and 'cast into the river or roughly buried under the end of Bow Bridge'. Baldwin clarified this point by explicitly – and correctly – attributing it to John Speede.

Like Strange, Edwards and many other researchers, Baldwin believed that Richard III 'was buried in the church of the Grey Friars',[56] although he produced no new evidence to back up this belief. His paper concluded:

> It is possible (though perhaps now unlikely) that at some time in the twenty-first century an excavator may yet reveal the slight remains of this famous monarch; but in the meantime we can do no more than agree with Charles Billson that **the grave most probably lies beneath the northern (St Martin's) end of Grey Friars Street, or the buildings that face it on either side**'.[57]

In the light of David Baldwin's very clear statement as to his view of the likely burial site, it is hard to understand on what basis the University of Leicester should maintain that Baldwin identified Richard's burial place as *the Social Services car park* – a location which lies well to the west of Grey Friars street and its adjacent buildings. Especially as Audrey Strange (1975) and W.J. White (1978), as cited above, *correctly identified his grave site as a car park* in the decade before Baldwin's article was written.

---

[52] W.J. White, 'Changing Burial Practice in Late Mediaeval England', *The Ricardian*, Vol. IV No. 63 (December 1978), p. 28.

[53] D. Baldwin, 'King Richard's Grave in Leicester', *Transactions of Leicestershire Archaeological and Historical Society*, Vol. 60, 1986, pp. 21–4.

[54] *Op. cit.*, p. 24, fn. 5.

[55] *Op. cit.*, pp. 21–2.

[56] *Op. cit.*, p. 23.

[57] *Op. cit.*, p. 24, emphasis added. See C.J. Billson, *Mediaeval Leicester* (1920), p. 184: 'If then the Grey Friars' Church and the burial place of Richard III were in Robert Herrick's garden, Richard's remains must now lie, if undisturbed, somewhere beneath the Grey Friars Street or the buildings that face it. The exact place cannot be more nearly identified.'

For good measure another authority, of whom David Baldwin must also have been aware, was Jeremy Potter of the Richard III Society, who wrote in 1983 (*Good King Richard?* p. 268): 'all trace of the house of the Greyfriars where [Richard] was buried has been obliterated, his place of interment now a car park.' Potter was Chairman when the Society raised £20,000 for the celebrated statue by James Butler, RA, donated to the city of Leicester and unveiled at a civic ceremony in Castle Gardens in 1980. Information has recently come to light that Jeremy Potter had sought to encourage excavation of the car park area in the 1980s, as indeed had Audrey Strange in the 1960s, but both approaches had been unsuccessful.

The Richard III Society as an organization, although still interested in discussing his grave, remained unengaged as regards any pro-active moves aimed at pinpointing Richard's burial place or locating his remains. After the turn of the century there were individual members, e.g. Michael Marshall (2001)[58] who hoped to instigate a search, although his thoughts were centred mainly on the river Soar; also local archaeologist Carol Simmonds (2003)[59] laid out a coherent analysis of the difficulties inherent in such a search, whether at the Greyfriars or in the river Soar, describing how archaeological investigations would probably be conducted, and suggesting the Society should approach the Leicestershire County Archaeologist. She cited a 1999 article by Dr David Treybig of the Richard III Society's American Branch who was working on a project to identify the Greyfriars precinct with the aid of maps from mediaeval times to the present day.[60] Like many who were prepared to countenance heretical views, Dr Treybig used cautious language: 'there is no empirical evidence to prove incorrect the view that his grave may yet lie, unmarked, somewhere on these premises.'

Interestingly, Dr Treybig's article was drawn to the attention of John Ashdown-Hill for clarification of the map drawn by John Speede, which in turn led Ashdown-Hill to review the map and ultimately identify Speede's error and its consequences.

Much ink was expended on speculation as to the possibility of retrieving remains from the river, and letters to the *Ricardian Bulletin* from William J. White and Geoffrey Wheeler[61] emphasized the inherent difficulties, Dr White explaining that if exposed to the running water of the river all the DNA would have disappeared over time. He still saw no reason, however, to credit the story of the grave desecration, and preferred to think that opportunities might exist to investigate the Greyfriars area. 'It would be unduly pessimistic,' he believed, 'to write off the possibility that archaeological excavation of the Leicester Grey Friars would be informative.' Despite extensive building on the site, he felt that Scheduled Ancient Monument status would provide protection against further development.

Geoffrey Wheeler drew attention to an article in the local *Leicester Mercury* newspaper[62] to which David Baldwin contributed, where University of Leicester specialists in osteology and genetics were quite bullish about the degree of success achievable in investigating any human remains that might be discovered. The article centred around whether any of the skulls which had been found in the river Soar might belong to Richard III. Thus interest in Leicester was still heavily mired in the story of the 'bones in the river', although Baldwin tried (and sadly failed) to steer readers away from this lurid tale by suggesting that the former king's remains might still lie where he was buried: 'somewhere close to the former NatWest bank in Greyfriars Lane [*sic*] ... under those well trodden streets towards St Martin's. We will never be certain, of course, unless we excavate the whole area. I don't think there is much prospect of finding him, but you never know. Stranger things have happened.'

---

[58] M. Marshall, 'Richard's remains need to be recovered', *Ricardian Bulletin* (December 2001), pp. 63-6.
[59] C. Simmonds, 'The Bare bones of Dissent', *Ricardian Bulletin* (Summer 2003), pp. 39-43.
[60] D. Treybig, 'In Search of Greyfriars', *Ricardian Register*, Vol. XXIV No. 1 (Spring 1999).
[61] *Ricardian Bulletin* (December 2002), pp. 67-71.
[62] A. Wakelin, 'Focus', *Leicester Mercury*, 8 October 2002, p. 10.

In the same year a book was published by local resident Ken Wright about the Bosworth battlefield,[63] tentatively agreeing with Baldwin that Richard's remains might not have been thrown into the Soar; that being the case, they might still lie 'very close to Grey Friars street. ... an approximation would be immediately to the west of the present day street called "The Grey Friars" and towards its northern end'. He accompanied this with a sketch-plan indicating an area lying, like Baldwin's, underneath buildings which would render it inaccessible to excavation (Fig. 9).

Despite this flurry of interest there was no move on the part of the university or any Leicester historians or archaeologists aimed at pursuing thoughts of actually mounting a search. The reason was probably because the published sites of both Baldwin and Wright were either metalled or built over.

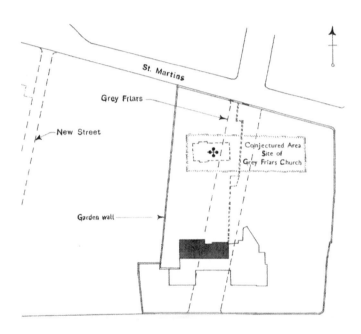

Fig. 9: Detail of plan (redrawn) suggested by Ken Wright (2002) showing the church lying under the road and buildings of the present-day Grey Friars street, to the east of the car parks. This was also the approximate location of the church according to David Baldwin.

---

[63] K. Wright, *The Field of Bosworth* (Leicester, 2002).

27

5
DNA of Richard III and his Siblings

On 25–27 September 2003 the *Centre Européen d'Etudes Bourgignonnes* held its 44th annual conference at Mechelen in Belgium. This conference was in commemoration of the 500th anniversary of the death of Margaret of York, Duchess of Burgundy, the youngest surviving sister of Edward IV and Richard III. Margaret, as dowager Duchess of Burgundy, had her palace in Mechelen where part of the building survives. She died on 23 November 1503. At her own request her body was buried at the Franciscan Priory (*De Minder-Broeders*) in Mechelen. She was *'begraven in den inganck van de Choor'* (buried at the entrance to the choir)[64] – a site which, as we now know, so closely reflects the grave-site of her brother, Richard III, in the Franciscan Priory in Leicester, that Margaret's choice of this specific location, and in her local Franciscan Priory, is unlikely to have been coincidental.

Subsequently the *Minder-Broeders* suffered from the religious conflicts in the Low Countries. The church was sacked by Elizabeth I's soldiers in the sixteenth century and used as stables by the troops of Napoleon I in the nineteenth century. By the twentieth century the priory had been dissolved and the remains of its building were transformed into a cultural centre. Meanwhile all trace of Margaret of York's tomb had been lost.

The conference included a presentation by Dr Paul De Win on three sets of female bones which had been found in the choir of Mechelen's former Franciscan Priory Church, in a position generally consistent with Margaret's reported tomb site. Additionally, they all appeared to belong to individuals whose age at death was close to hers. The ensuing discussion focused on how it might possibly be ascertained whether or not any of the remains really were those of Margaret of York. It was proposed by Dr John Ashdown-Hill (a member of the Society of Genealogists, who had already published genetically and genealogically based research on the house of Lancaster, Lady Eleanor Talbot and her family, Elizabeth Lucy, and the missing molars of Anne Mowbray) to seek a mtDNA sequence for Margaret of York and her siblings.

From exploration of the female-line ancestry of Margaret of York it emerged that this could not be traced further back than Margaret's great grandmother, Catherine de Roët (Swynford), because the identity of Catherine's mother was not on record. It thus emerged that the only possible sources of a relevant all-female line of descent must be focused on Catherine de Roët and her sister, Philippa (Chaucer). Since Philippa's daughter had become a nun, this restricted the lines of descent to the daughters and female-line granddaughters of Catherine's only daughter, Joan Beaufort, Countess of Westmorland. Dr Ashdown-Hill then attempted to trace all such lines.

The simplest line to trace was that of Anne of York, Duchess of Exeter (sister of Margaret of York, Edward IV and Richard III, all grandchildren of Joan Beaufort), because a full record

---

[64] J.F. Gislenus Cuypers van Alsinghen, *Provincie, Stad, Ende District Van Mechelen*, vol. 2 (1770), p. 3.

of her descendants had been published in the early twentieth century.[65] From this published account Ashdown-Hill was able to extract one all-female line of descent down to Barbara Gough, b. 21 March 1747, who had married Isaac Spooner in 1770.[66] Using a variety of modern genealogical sources, including birth records, marriage records and wills, he then extended this line of descent from Barbara Gough through her daughter, Anne Spooner, to the latter's daughter, Charlotte Vansittart Neale. Charlotte eventually proved to be the all-female line great-grandmother of Muriel Joyce Brown (aka Joy Ibsen), who was still living in Canada in 2004. Ashdown-Hill contacted Mrs Ibsen in April 2004, and in May she agreed to give a sample for DNA analysis, but requested that until and unless she gave permission, details of her mtDNA sequence should not be published. In June 2004 Joy's sample was sent to Oxford Ancestors together with a consent letter allowing them to reveal the results to Ashdown-Hill, and for him to forward them to colleagues in Belgium. The work was designated as 'Special Project R13251'. On 11 August 2004, Joy Ibsen acknowledged receipt of her mtDNA sequence results (haplogroup J) from Oxford Ancestors.

Despite the fact that written records provided a continuous and all-female line of descent from Anne of York, Duchess of Exeter to Joy Ibsen, written records are not always accurate. Therefore, in an attempt to confirm Joy Ibsen's mtDNA sequence as that of Margaret of York and her siblings, Dr Ashdown-Hill was concerned to find either another all-female line living descendant, or a source of dead DNA from the same family. Since tracing another all-female line living descendant proved difficult, he sought a dead DNA sample, and for this purpose he contacted the Ashmolean Museum in Oxford to request strands of hair which had been taken from Edward IV's coffin in the eighteenth century and presented to the museum by the Dean of Windsor.

In addition he tried to trace the present location of an arm of Cecily Neville's uncle, Thomas Beaufort, Duke of Exeter, extracted when the duke's body was exhumed from Bury St Edmunds Abbey ruins in the eighteenth century, and held at one time by the Royal College of Surgeons in London. However, it seemed that this arm was destroyed during the Second World War bombing of London.

He published news of the initial discovery of the putative mtDNA sequence of Margaret of York and her siblings (including Richard III) in 2005 in the *Medelai Gazette* ('Finding the DNA of Richard III', vol. 12, no. 2, August 2005, pp. 13-14), and in *Your Family Tree*, 28 ('The bones of Margaret of York', September 2005), pp. 28-30; and subsequently in 'Alive and Well in Canada – the Mitochondrial DNA of Richard III', *The Ricardian* Vol. XVI (2006), pp. 1-14. On p. 4 of this article he also revealed that the Somerset family of the Duke of Beaufort could potentially establish the Plantagenet male-line DNA (Y-chromosome).

On 25 April 2005, samples had been taken from the three sets of putative Margaret of York female bones found in Mechelen, for DNA testing against new samples from Joy Ibsen. This new testing was conducted by Professor Cassiman of the Catholic University of Leuven, but the results, received eventually in 2006, were disappointing: two of the sets of female bones from Mechelen were found not to match Joy Ibsen's mtDNA. The third set produced a confused (contaminated) result.

Although the Mechelen project had apparently proved unsuccessful, the fact that Richard III's putative mtDNA had been found was welcomed by Ricardian scholars. In May 2006 Ashdown-Hill gave a presentation on his discovery before HRH The Duke of Gloucester at the Richard III Society Staples' Inn Reception. The following month he contacted the Duke of Beaufort outlining the possible Y-chromosome research, and requesting a DNA sample, but on

---

[65] M.A.H.D. de Ruvigny, *The Plantagenet Roll of the Blood Royal*, 5 volumes (1903-1911), volume 3 *Exeter* (1906).

[66] *Ibid.*, p. 657.

16 June the Duke of Beaufort replied that he was 'not interested in participating'. Since the work on the (female) Mechelen bones could not make use of Y-chromosome information there was no point in pursuing the male-line Plantagenet DNA at this point, beyond establishing that there were a number of male relatives of the Duke of Beaufort who might also be able to give suitable samples at some stage for this purpose.

Towards the end of 2006 an Edward IV hair sample was finally received from the Ashmolean Museum in Oxford. It was hoped this would confirm that Joy Ibsen's mtDNA was that of Edward IV, Richard III and their sisters Anne and Margaret. In March 2007 the Edward IV sample was delivered to Professor Cassiman at the Catholic University of Leuven for testing. However, it proved impossible to extract a mtDNA sequence from this hair.

The year 2007 also saw the publication, with Joy Ibsen's permission, of full details of Richard III's mtDNA sequence in respect of HVR1 and HVR2 (exactly as subsequently found in the Leicester bones in 2013), in 'Margaret of York's Dance of Death — the DNA evidence', *Handelingen van de Koninklijke Kring voor Oudheidkunde, Letteren an Kunst van Mechelen*, 111 2007, 193-207. In this paper, Ashdown-Hill concluded provisionally that the Mechelen bones were not those of Margaret of York, with the clearly expressed reservation that confirmation of Joy Ibsen's DNA sequence was still required. Sadly, the following year Joy Ibsen herself died of cancer (November 2008).

Ashdown-Hill had meanwhile been preparing a new book, *The Last Days of Richard III*, containing details of the mtDNA discovery (The History Press, first edition published 2010). It also included a family tree showing details of the Y-chromosome descent, and reported that the Duke of Beaufort had declined to give a sample – but that other living male members of his family remained as potential sources.

Because the existence of a probable mtDNA sequence for Richard III offered the chance of identifying his remains, this would prove to be a major factor when it was used by Philippa Langley in persuading the authorities in Leicester to agree to a search for the king's lost grave.

In August 2012, when Langley's archaeological dig was launched, Ashdown-Hill's mtDNA research for Richard III was made available to Dr Turi King, geneticist at the University of Leicester, who obtained a new living DNA sample from Joy Ibsen's elder son, Michael. Subsequent DNA work post-dated the discovery of Richard III's remains, but to complete the story it will be summarized briefly here.

On 21-22 September Dr Ashdown-Hill offered Dr King full details of his Plantagenet Y-chromosome research, including a list of ten living male members of the Somerset family, located in South Africa and in various parts of England and Australia. She replied that this would be a very exciting second line of DNA research to pursue, and one in which she had specific expertise. At her request, Ashdown-Hill then supplied her with the list of names and addresses he had prepared, and consented to her contacting them 'under the banner of the University of Leicester' to request DNA samples.

At the same time a team led by Professor Kevin Schürer of the University of Leicester finally found a second all-female line living descendant whose mtDNA confirmed the sequence of Joy Ibsen as that of Richard III and his siblings.

On 4 February 2013 Dr Turi King officially announced that the bones found in Leicester had mtDNA which matched that of Joy Ibsen and her son Michael.

6
Inception of the Search for Richard III

As the first decade of the new century drew to a close, a great deal of material had been amassed by Ricardian scholars which would contribute to finding and identifying Richard III if his grave were to be located.

- His last resting place had been confirmed, by reference to the most credible records and memorials, as the Franciscan Priory Church in Leicester.
- The report of John Rous – himself a fifteenth-century priest – that Richard had been buried 'in the choir of the church', had been established as entirely appropriate to the circumstances.
- Despite many traditional historians clinging to the story that his remains had been removed (a story discounted as early as 1844 by Halsted), this had now been satisfactorily refuted by John Ashdown-Hill.
- The extensive area of the Greyfriars precinct was already known: it remained only to locate the priory church (covering a relatively small area).
- Scientific tests were available (DNA matching, carbon dating, isotope testing, etc.), should remains be found which required identification.

The view of a few progressive twentieth-century Ricardians, e.g. Audrey Strange, Bill White and Jeremy Potter, had been that Richard's grave lay under the present-day parking areas around the location of the Leicester council offices. This view was shared by Ashdown-Hill, who brought to the subject his thorough knowledge and understanding of how the Franciscan friars laid out their priories. This knowledge led him to conclude that the parking area was the ideal place to excavate for the site of the priory church, the main part of which was likely to lie under the tarmac, not under the later buildings around the edges of the site.

Screenwriter Philippa Langley, founder and long-time secretary of the Richard III Society's Scottish Branch, was following her own lines of investigation in connection with a biographical Richard III screenplay, and had made her own visits to Leicester in the late spring of 2004 and 2005 where she inspected the parking areas of the Greyfriars site. Convinced that proper investigation of the site of the Social Services car park at its northern end could and should be undertaken, she embarked on archival research which included reading Audrey Strange *et al.* She identified three key questions that needed to be answered before any search for the king's grave could begin:[67]

1. How could Richard be identified if found?
2. Was his body there or had he been thrown into the river Soar as mainstream accounts believed?
3. Where was the location of the small priory church within the extensive Greyfriars precinct area?

---

[67] P. Langley & M. Jones, *The King's Grave* (2013), pp. 7-8.

Hearing of John Ashdown-Hill's DNA breakthrough in autumn 2005, Langley realized that the first of her three obstacles had been overcome. She contacted Ashdown-Hill and urged him to make use of the facilities offered by television, specifically the Channel 4 *Time Team* archaeology series, and in October 2005 he wrote to the production company suggesting a search in Leicester at the site of the Social Services car park which he identified in a photograph (Fig. 2): (a) to clarify the layout of the conventual buildings, and (b) to possibly find the remains of Richard III (which, if successful, could be identified with the help of Joy Ibsen's mitochondrial DNA sequence). The suggestion was regretfully turned down owing to the size of the car park area, which would be beyond the programme's three-day time frame; but the partnership had been forged which would eventually achieve those very outcomes.

Meanwhile Annette Carson, who would become another member of the retrieval and reburial project, had been independently researching and writing on the life and reign of Richard III. In 2008 she published *Richard III: The Maligned King*, which was welcomed by Ashdown-Hill and Langley as a fresh and thorough study of how his reign was illuminated by contemporary sources, rather than relying on the widely accepted traditional accounts coloured by bias, fable and Elizabethan theatre. Carson roundly rejected the improbable stories of the bones in the river and the coffin as horse-trough: 'As for his body,' she wrote, 'there is no reason to doubt that it remained where the friars buried it. ... The site would probably now lie beneath the private car park of the Department of Social Services.'[68] On her return to England after living abroad she was invited to join the team by Langley whose work on setting up the search was already far advanced.

Thus it was only a small group of Ricardians – historians, researchers and writers – who considered the evidence sufficiently compelling to pinpoint this specific site as the king's burial place and worthy of investigation, a project which Langley would now devote years of time and effort to bring about.

Regrettably, in view of subsequent events, it needs to be emphasized that no other persons or institutions worked to amass the evidence needed to launch such a project, nor did anyone in Leicester instigate the idea of mounting a search for the king's grave. The reason for this is simple: they lacked the necessary knowledge and incentive. First, work of this nature has always lain in the hands of researchers and historians whom academics (and recently even archaeologists) have been pleased to call 'amateurs'. Second, almost the entire population of Leicester and its archaeologists believed the unlikely tradition that the grave had been desecrated and destroyed. And third, the very small number of local people who considered the grave might still be intact (including David Baldwin and Ken Wright) believed it to lie under inaccessible roads and buildings.[69] They were therefore uninterested when the media announced that Ashdown-Hill had traced the mtDNA which could significantly assist in identifying Richard III if he were ever to be found.

The response from *Time Team* was a setback, and Langley was aware of no other proposals for an archaeological dig. However, with the support of her own Scottish Branch, and in particular the treasurer, Dr Raymond Bord, she continued assembling materials relevant to the Greyfriars site. In late summer 2007 an archaeological investigation took place prior to a proposed demolition in Grey Friars street, under a building at the extreme east of the presumed Greyfriars precinct: the precise area, in fact, which Baldwin and Wright projected as the site of the church. Nothing of significance was found, and the dig was dismissed locally as of little importance (see section 7, 'Local Topography and Archaeology'). For Langley the opposite was

---

[68] A. Carson, *Richard III: The Maligned King* (2008/2009), pp. 269-70; Langley & Jones, *The King's Grave* (2013) p.10.
[69] See footnote 57 above.

the case.[70] Realizing that their results suggested a location farther west for the church, she pursued enquiries with the city council's archaeologist and as a result obtained a much clearer picture of her area of interest. Soon afterwards her researches turned up a plan of mediaeval Leicester[71] on which she found for the first time a clear depiction of the Church of the Franciscan Priory (16 on plan) located adjacent to the road at the north of the priory precinct. Equally importantly, it was drawn almost immediately across the road from the Church of St Martin's which survives today as Leicester Cathedral (14 on plan). The site it occupied strongly resembled the site of the Social Services car park (Fig. 10).

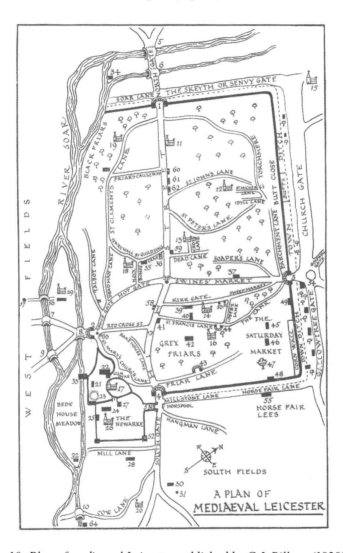

Fig. 10: Plan of mediaeval Leicester published by C.J. Billson (1920).

---

[70] Langley & Jones, *The King's Grave*, pp. 9-10.
[71] Illustrations in Strange (1975) and Simmonds (2003) led to Langley locating this plan in C.J. Billson, *Mediaeval Leicester*, p. xiii.

Further research seemed to confirm this view that the priory church and grave could be situated directly to the south of St Martin's Church/Leicester Cathedral. The 1791 *Histories and Antiquities of the Ancient Town of Leicester* by John Throsby included a 'Plan of Leicester' which had very little marked in its centre other than St Martin's Church and the location of the king's grave (see Fig. 11).

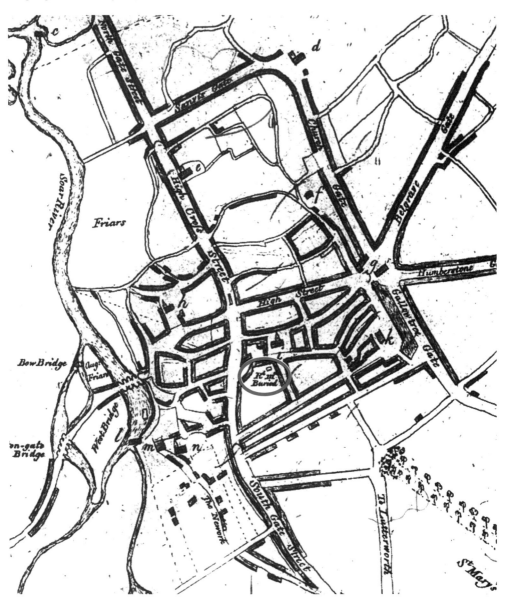

Fig. 11: Detail from plan of Leicester published by John Throsby (1791/2) showing 'R^d III Buried'. Reproduced by permission of National Library of Scotland.

Although the grave was shown as being situated under the buildings directly to the west of the newly laid out New Street, it nevertheless gave further credence to this area being the potential

34

site of the priory church. Throsby's text also seemed to confirm this view: *'The FRANCISCAN or GREY FRIARY, stood on the South side of St. Martin's church-yard,*[72] towards which there is a portal remaining; but the other building is quite demolished, most of it now belongs to Mr. Noble, who has a very fine house.'[73] (Emphasis added.)

Looking to see whether this could be confirmed in other plans, Langley now returned to two articles written by the American researcher Dr David Treybig in 1999 and 2000.[74] In a quest to locate the Greyfriars precinct, Treybig had found no indication in modern maps and had turned instead to maps charting development since the eighteenth century. These showed that the present-day areas used as car parks across the road south of the cathedral had remained undeveloped through the years. An area to the west of New Street had originally been a garden, and a 1955 map marked it with a cross and the word 'Ruin' (see also section 7, 'Local Topography and Archaeology'). To the left were the words 'Franciscan Friary (site of)'. This site would clearly need to be included within Langley's proposed investigation, for which Ground Penetrating Radar (GPR) would be a necessary pre-requisite with its ability to indicate any potential sub-surface structures and other archaeological features.

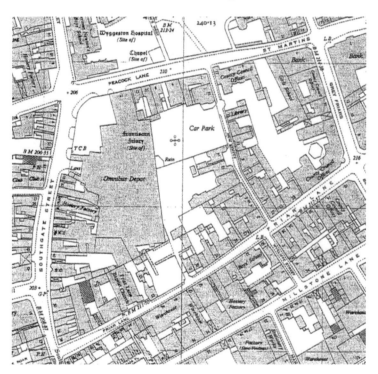

Fig. 12: 1955 Ordnance Survey map of the area showing a cross and the marker 'Ruin' in New Street car park.

---

[72] Confirmed also by Billson, pp. 78–9: 'The priory and church stood on the south side of St. Martin's churchyard … One of the Gateways opened on Friar Lane, and there was another entrance from what is now called Peacock Lane.' *Cf.* J. Nichols, *Bibliotheca Topographica Britannica* No. 7 VII (1782) p. 601.

[73] John Throsby, *Histories and Antiquities of the Ancient Town of Leicester* (1791), p. 290, citing 'Mr Carte' – certainly Rev. Samuel Carte, *Essay on the Antiquities and History of Leicester* (1721) which directly refers to this (not Thomas Carte's well known *General History of England* published 1747-55).

[74] David L. Treybig, PhD, 'In Search of Greyfriars', *Ricardian Register,* journal of the Richard III Society's American Branch (Spring 1999, Spring 2000).

More convinced than ever that an archaeological dig should be attempted, along with a prior GPR survey, Langley organized a Richard III Society Scottish Branch study day held on 21 February 2009, at which she invited Ashdown-Hill to give a series of keynote talks on his discovery of Richard III's mtDNA and his research into Richard's burial. At this time they also exchanged views on the 'bones in the river' story. Langley had been impressed by Audrey Strange's suggestion that somehow the desecration of John Wycliffe's grave had become wrongly identified with that of Richard III. She now learned that Ashdown-Hill was about to publish his findings to the effect that John Speede had failed to find Richard's grave owing to the simple error of looking in the wrong place, which had then been compounded by his spreading the tale of the 'jeering mob'.[75] This convincing proof that the story was a myth had now overcome the second of Langley's three obstacles.

When they met they realized that by different routes they had also reached the same conclusion about the third question that must be answered. i.e. the location of the lost Franciscan Priory Church. This, and hence potentially Richard's grave, must be situated in the northern end of the Social Services car park. At Edinburgh's Cramond Inn, during the luncheon break of the study day, which John Ashdown-Hill had entitled 'Honour My Bones', Philippa Langley launched the Looking For Richard Project.

Also present were Dr David Johnson and his wife Wendy, both long-standing members of the Richard III Society. At Langley's suggestion they made a renewed attempt at contacting the TV programme *Time Team*, but to no avail. Shortly afterwards, also at Langley's suggestion, Ashdown-Hill attempted to interest ULAS, the local archaeology contractors in Leicester, about a search for the king's grave, but received no response.

To become a coherent operation, the search had to encompass many facets. There were practical aspects (permissions, funding, technical expertise, etc.); and there were ethical considerations (plans had to be prepared for the proper treatment and ultimate reburial of the king's remains, if found). There needed to be a guiding principle, and so the ethos of the search was conceived:

> *Richard III was first and foremost a human being, and an individual who has living relatives today. He was also a member of the royal family, and as the anointed King of England he was a former Head of State. The ethos of the Looking For Richard project was to search for, recover, and rebury his mortal remains with the honour, dignity and respect so conspicuously denied following his death at the battle of Bosworth.*

In practical terms, Langley's plan of the search would involve all three car parks – the remaining open spaces – within the Greyfriars precinct area. Focusing on the Social Services car park, the central area situated directly opposite Leicester Cathedral (mediaeval St Martin's Church), the investigation would also include the New Street car park (to the west) and the former grammar school car park (to the east), see Fig. 13 below.

The search for the king's grave would require:

1. Permission from the three car park owners to undertake a Ground Penetrating Radar Survey (GPR) of their land in order to attempt to locate the walls of the priory church and / or its ancillary buildings and any potential grave sites beneath the tarmac.
2. Permission from Leicester City Council, owners of the Social Services car park, for an archaeological investigation of their land.

---

[75] J. Ashdown-Hill, *The Last Days of Richard III* (2010), p. 134; (2013), p. 157.

3. Permission from William Davis Ltd, owners of the former grammar school car park, for an archaeological investigation of this land also.
4. Commissioning of an archaeological unit willing to undertake the work, and cost it.
5. Funding for the GPR survey, and subsequent archaeological investigation.
6. Identifying Richard III, should he be found, and making arrangements for his honourable reburial.

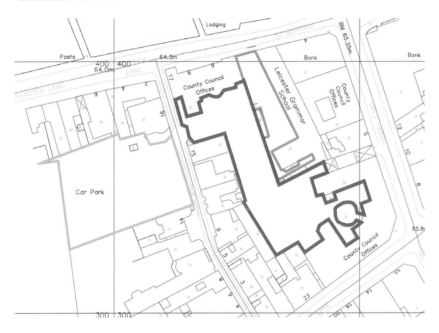

Fig. 13: Outlines of the three car parks to be surveyed by GPR,
Social Services car park in the centre (June 2011).

In the worst recession in living memory, it was clear that the project needed something powerful to focus local attention and bring in the funding. Working in film and TV, Langley would bring in television.

Ashdown-Hill was now completing *'The Last Days of Richard III'*; Langley would wait for its publication (in July 2010). Having now made progress with the TV industry (see section 8, 'Facilitation'), in August 2010 the project was ready to be pitched to Leicester City Council. The council confirmed their interest in September. Desk-based research by Langley with UK archaeological units had revealed that archaeological best practice was to rebury human remains as close as possible to the site of discovery, therefore this pattern was followed in the pitch document, with Leicester Cathedral named as the proposed place of reburial.

Because of their respective skills, Langley commissioned historian Dr Johnson and artist Wendy Johnson to design a tomb for King Richard. The production of a tomb design would emphasize the seriousness with which all aspects of the search, and potential consequences, were being addressed. Accordingly the Johnsons put together the Reburial Document, a wide ranging proposal incorporating the tomb design, detailed suggestions for the commemorative process, and the ethos underpinning the project (see below – Section 10, 'Reburial and Commemoration' and Appendix 1).

At the end of 2010, the city council confirmed to Langley the verbal agreement that the project would be allowed to proceed on the basis that, should the king be found, he would be reburied in Leicester Cathedral. Other places had been mentioned but not pursued: these included Westminster Abbey and St Mary de Castro in Leicester.

In early 2011 details of the project together with the Reburial Document were given to the Ministry of Justice,[76] the office of HRH The Duke of Gloucester and the Royal Coroner. An important precedent had to be considered, i.e. the discovery of Anne Mowbray's remains, which was cited within the documentation for the project.[77]

The Ministry of Justice stipulated two important points: that whatever arrangements were required for the retrieval and reburial of Richard III must first be put in place *locally*, as these would then be passed for implementation into any exhumation licence; also that a licence application for the exhumation of a named individual of this antiquity (with living collateral descendants) was relatively unusual and there would be 'greater sensitivities to weigh up'.[78]

In March 2011 the local archaeology contractors ULAS had agreed to be commissioned for the project subject to being first engaged to undertake a preliminary map regression analysis of the car park areas to assess the viability of excavating there. For this they were given the information which Langley had assembled from the prior research of herself and others,[79] which was later incorporated into the ULAS report. Richard Buckley, co-director, looked at the change in land use over time and identified Thomas Roberts's map of 1741 (Fig. 14). This showed the 'Gray Fryers' area directly opposite St. Martin's Church (Leicester Cathedral), and with the area which Langley determined to be Herrick's garden situated farther to the east. If Herrick's last known memorial to the king's grave from 1612 was indeed correct, this would possibly lie within the former grammar school car park (see further investigations, section 7, 'Local Topography and Archaeology'). The project was well on track, and Langley continued drawing up plans to discuss with the council and cathedral.

By June, Leicester Cathedral had received the Looking For Richard Project details together with the Reburial Document which included the initial tomb design now enhanced with computer assisted drawings of the tomb in plan and elevation. The cathedral authorities

---

[76] Email from Philippa Langley to Robert Clifford, Head of Burials Team, Coroners and Burials Division, *'Looking For Richard: In Search of a King'* (11 January 2011), *inter alia*: 'After his defeat at Bosworth, he [Richard] was buried in the choir of the Greyfriars Church in Leicester. With the dissolution of the monasteries the building fell into disrepair and his grave forgotten /lost. A story was then put about that King Richard's bones had been thrown into the River Soar. Research has revealed this story to be erroneous and that King Richard's remains could still lay within the original site, an area that is now considered to be that of an open air car park.'

[77] Its relevance related to the accidental discovery in 1964 of the remains of this young royal princess (died 1481), consort of Edward IV's younger son, Richard, Duke of York. Her body was accidentally discovered on a building site in London and then subjected, without consent, to investigation and media publicity. Questions were asked in the House of Lords, including Lord Amulree's subsequent enquiry 'whether it is proposed that the same rather cumbersome procedure will be followed when the body of a Royal or a noble person is unexpectedly found in the course of some kind of excavation?' (http://hansard.millbanksystems.com/lords/1966/aug/09/remains-of-anne-mowbray-duchess-of-york). In the case of Anne Mowbray, her living – but very remote – collateral descendants took steps via the House of Lords to close down any further investigation and secure an honourable reburial for the princess at Westminster Abbey.

[78] Email from Robert Clifford, Head of Burials Team, Coroners and Burials Division, to Philippa Langley, 12 January 2011, *inter alia*: 'It is relatively unusual to have a licence application in relation to the remains of a named person of this age, and therefore with potential descendants, so this would raise greater sensitivities to weigh up, even if the remains were not royal. You are, of course, already well seized of this.'

[79] *'The Greyfriars, Leicester'* (see footnote 101).

confirmed their willingness to give Richard III an honourable reburial should he be found, taking account of his Catholicism. Darlow Smithson TV Productions were now also on board and Channel 4 had cautiously confirmed their interest.

The archaeology package as outlined by ULAS included the services of their unit's Senior Officer and Project Osteologist, Harriet Jacklyn, whose expertise Langley took the precaution to research to ensure her experience embraced not only modern bones but also, crucially, remains that dated from antiquity. The contractual fees provided that one set of human remains would be afforded full analysis by ULAS with the objective of establishing their identity (see below – Costs Breakdown, Appendix 3).

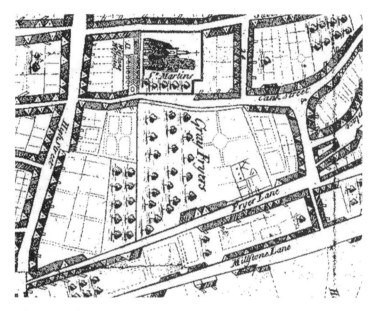

Fig 14: Thomas Roberts map 1741 showing Robert Herrick's garden laid out on east side of an orchard.

DNA was a primary topic of discussion now that Ashdown-Hill had established that, following the death of Joy Ibsen in 2008, a sample could be donated by her elder son, Michael Ibsen, Richard III's seventeenth-generation nephew. Langley knew of the global reputation of the genetics department of the University of Leicester for its pioneering work in genetic fingerprinting, therefore approaches were made to Dr Turi King, Lecturer in Genetics and Archaeology. She agreed that if human remains were found which showed potential for being compatible with those of Richard III, she could arrange to conduct tests to retrieve a mtDNA sample and attempt to match it with Michael Ibsen's mtDNA comparator.

At Buckley's suggestion the university's Head of Corporate Affairs, Richard Taylor, was brought in to meet Langley. He was enthusiastic about the archaeology project and immediately agreed to provide facilities for the DNA matching if a potential candidate should be discovered. He asked if there was any other way the university could assist, and agreed to Langley's suggestion for Professor Mark Lansdale, Head of the Psychology Department, to pursue a psychological evaluation of Richard III.[80]

---

[80] Prof. Lansdale and Dr Julian Boon, the department's inventor of personality profiling, had previously expressed interest to Langley in the concept of retrospectively analysing Richard III and went on to produce an unprecedented personality profile for the search project; this was one of several items proposed

By July 2011, the Written Scheme of Investigation (WSI) for the final archaeology project had been agreed between Langley as the client and Buckley representing the contractors ULAS. The document enshrined in writing a raft of provisions covering every aspect of the proposed dig from safety measures to equipment to the restitution of the tarmac when it was concluded. It also served as the written instrument for recording (on the advice of the Ministry of Justice) those careful arrangements which Langley had mutually agreed in advance with ULAS, Leicester City Council and the Royal Household covering sensitive topics in the event of a discovery that could prove to be Richard III: such as the degree to which his remains would be protected from public view and media photography, and how long they would be available to ULAS for the agreed necessary identification processes. In relation to the care of such remains, it confirmed Langley's status as custodian responsible for their transfer to a chapel of rest prior to arrival at the cathedral for obsequies and reburial.

The WSI was submitted to Leicester City Council who approved its contents; its official acceptance was recorded in the council's written permission, issued to Langley in early August, for her proposed survey of the car park by Ground Penetrating Radar (GPR) as well as the proposed subsequent archaeological investigation (for both agreements see Appendix 4). Langley had also taken the precaution of approaching the owners of the other car parks seeking permission for archaeological investigations to take place. Only the private owner of the New Street car park declined.

Later that same month, with funding from private investors and individual members of the Richard III Society, Langley arranged the preliminary GPR survey of the three car parks (see section 7, 'Local Topography and Archaeology'). One of the principal donors was the Society's Chairman, Dr Phil Stone, a member of the Looking For Richard Project team whose support was to prove crucial over the project's lifetime and would rescue it on a number of occasions.

The GPR survey results would also help the ULAS team to decide upon the layout of the trenches: the contract called for three trenches in all, the first two for the investigation of the primary area, the Social Services car park, with a later third trench intended, at this stage, for the adjacent school car park, which appeared to offer possibilities as evidenced in Roberts's map.

A year later, after overcoming a succession of problems including shortfalls in financial support, the ground was eventually cut on 25 August 2012.

for the Channel 4 documentary which never reached the screen. Prof. Lansdale and Dr Boon published their work in the *Ricardian Bulletin* (March 2013), pp. 46-56. See also Langley & Jones, *The King's Grave* (2013), p. 254.

7
Local Topography and Archaeology

Leicester's archaeological narrative is largely dominated by its Roman past when it was known as *Ratæ Coritanorum*. By the early twenty-first century, following a considerable amount of redevelopment work and resultant archaeological examination of the city, it had revealed much of its mediaeval past.[81] Yet the Greyfriars precinct area in the south remained largely ignored by modern development and, as a result, archaeological investigation. Any attempt to interpret the location of the Franciscan Priory Church using Leicester's archaeological record had little to rely on.

Such had been the handicap experienced by the American researcher, Dr David Treybig, as mentioned above (see pages 26, 35) in seeking the location of the Greyfriars precinct. In two tourist maps of the city centre, freely available at the time from the University of Leicester (1999) and Leicester Promotions (1995), he found no mention of the Greyfriars area or indeed any sites reflecting the city's Ricardian associations.[82] Although a 'Richard III Trail' leaflet was located and supplied to him by the Richard III Society's archivist Geoffrey Wheeler, Treybig noted that enquiries for information about Richard III in Leicester itself yielded little result.

None the wiser, he turned instead to map regression analysis to see if this would offer a way forward. In his readings he was confused by John Speede's erroneous identification of the Dominican priory site as the Greyfriars (see above), and misled into believing that the eastern edge of the precinct was bounded by the street of Grey Friars, rather than its actual boundary farther east at Hotel Street;[83] but it was his research into the far west of the precinct area that held interest for Philippa Langley.

Treybig's maps charted the expansion of urbanisation within the Greyfriars area over a key period of 148 years from 1741 to 1889 which had left a number of centralized open spaces that would eventually become the modern day parking areas situated across the road south of Leicester Cathedral / St Martin's Church. Of special interest was the open area to the west of New Street where more recent maps highlighted an interesting feature. A map from 1930 showed a large area west of New Street as a garden, which by 1955 had become a car park. Within this was a place marked with a stylized cross, and a small area to the south-west corner marked 'Ruin'. Furthermore, directly to the west of this site there was an area above the Southgates bus depot ('Omnibus Depot') which was described as 'Franciscan Friary (site of)' (see Fig. 12 above). This area – the present-day New Street car park – would clearly need to be included within Langley's proposed investigation. Ground Penetrating Radar (GPR) could potentially indicate any archaeological features below the surface, and a GPR survey was

---

[81] Most notably the excavation of St Peter's Church and graveyard, Vaughan Way (2004-2006), 9 St Nicholas Place (2003) and the £4 million Highcross development (2005-2009). *Ex informatio* ULAS.

[82] David L. Treybig, PhD, 'In Search of Greyfriars', *Ricardian Register,* journal of the Richard III Society's American Branch (Spring 2000).

[83] Through a notation on the map of Grey Friars from 1889, Treybig also confused the construction of Grey Friars street (1872) with that of New Street (1740). See footnote 87 below.

accordingly factored into the project.[84]

More information came to light in the late summer of 2007 when an opportunity for archaeological investigation was offered by the demolition of a 1950s single-storey extension of the NatWest/Pares Bank site in the street known as Grey Friars, which ran north-south on the east side of the Greyfriars precinct. This building, situated to the north-east of the Department of Social Services, was located in the area favoured for the church by Baldwin and Wright (see Fig. 9 above), and any finds there could help elucidate whether their theory was viable. But the excavation yielded nothing of particular note and was seen locally as of little consequence. For details of anything that might prove relevant, Langley needed to access the publication of the results of the dig, and for this she persuaded the Richard III Society to approach Leicester's city archaeologist, Chris Wardle, on an official basis.[85] This subsequent knowledge offered a step forward for the search project.

Although the area to be investigated was small (15m x 15m, equivalent to 1.25 per cent of the total precinct area), no part of the friary church was discovered, only a 'fragment of a stone coffin lid ... found in a post mediaeval drain'. The conclusion was evident: the church of the Greyfriars was located elsewhere. As the excavation was in the north-east of the precinct, the church must be farther west, as Langley and Ashdown-Hill's research had postulated.

Using the example of the Franciscan priory in Lichfield,[86] Wardle's report established that the church and principal buildings of the Greyfriars would have similarly occupied only a small fraction of the total precinct site, with 'the rest of the area taken up by a graveyard, various outbuildings and extensive gardens'. Estimation of the Greyfriars site at 180m long x 130m wide (in the west) x 70m wide (in the east) approximated to the city council's calculation of 6.7 acres, or roughly the equivalent of five football fields. Looking at the sum total of this report, it seemed to Langley that archaeological investigation of the central open car park spaces, specifically the Social Services site (situated directly opposite Leicester Cathedral / St Martin's Church), still offered the only way forward.[87]

Concentrating on this area, she researched more of its history. The buildings surrounding the Social Services car park were Georgian, and the only indication of any discoveries of human remains during their construction came from a report by John Throsby in 1791:

> The grounds belonging to this Friary were spacious, and extended from the upper end of the Market-place to the Friar-lane meeting-house; much of which has been built on in my time. When the workmen were digging for the cellars, to the range of houses which face St. Martin's church, they cast up, I remember, many human bones; one skeleton lay entire: the Friary church probably stood there.[88]

Since St Martin's Church (now Leicester Cathedral) was directly opposite, Langley pursued enquiries with its archivist to determine if any of the human remains discovered during Throsby's time had been reburied there. Of particular interest was the 'one skeleton entire', in the hope that this reburial might have been recorded. But the cathedral could find no records of

---

[84] Later GPR survey of the 'Ruin' area in the New Street car park in August 2011 showed an area of complex responses 'possibly relating to buried rubble or disturbed ground', see GPR image Fig. 18.

[85] Chris Wardle, 'Archaeological Excavations at Grey Friars, Leicester', *Ricardian Bulletin* (Summer 2008), pp. 34-37.

[86] Following an extensive excavation in the 1920s, and subsequently confirmed in the 1990s (Wardle, 2008).

[87] From the report Langley was also able to establish exactly when the street now called Grey Friars was laid out: in 1872 Greyfriars House had been demolished to make way for it on the western side of Pares Bank. Later research confirmed that New Street was laid out in 1740.

[88] John Throsby, *History and Antiquities of the Ancient Town of Leicester* (1791), p. 291.

any such reburials from this time. If the Franciscan Priory Church had been situated directly on St Martin's Road where the houses had been built, and if this skeleton had been the king's, it was long since gone.

However, searching through Ricardian archives, Langley came across an article that seemed to counter Throsby's statement.[89] In this, Lorraine Pickering detailed a report from 29 May 1862 which indicated that no skeletons had ever been found on the Greyfriars site.[90] A skeleton had been found in the river Soar by workmen who had taken it to the surveyor's office, and Dr Henry Lankester (1825-1902), a local surgeon who went on to become an MP and Mayor of Leicester, had 'minutely' examined it and believed it to be a young male.[91]

Another important aspect to research was the record of burials known to have taken place within the Franciscan Priory Church during its long history. For purposes of elimination, should human remains be found which might show signs of being Richard III (e.g. displaying battle trauma), it was necessary to establish what could be expected in terms of other burials in the choir and, if possible, their identities. Records for the priory were scant but seemed to suggest a minimal number of burials within the high-status choir area. Benefactors and founders could certainly be expected to have been buried there; but it seemed the vow of poverty taken by the friars themselves, together with the aftermath of a treasonous rebellion by some of the order against Henry IV in 1402, might well have reduced the overall numbers.[92] The following list was compiled:

BURIALS IN THE [CHOIR OF] THE FRANCISCAN PRIORY CHURCH[93]

SIR WILLIAM MOTON of Peckleton (Sheriff 1174)[94] died	c.1230?
GILBERT LUENOR (Founder before 1230)[95]	c.1250?
ELLEN LUENOR (Wife of Gilbert)	c.1250?
JOHN PICKERING of Stampwick (Early benefactor)[96]	c.1250
HENRY DE RERESBY (Scottish Provincial)[97]	c.1250
PETER SWYNFELD (Provincial)	c.1271
WILLIAM OF NOTTINGHAM (Provincial)	c.1330
RICHARD III	1485

[89] Lorraine Pickering, *Medelai Gazette*, Richard III Foundation Inc. (November 2003), p. 18.

[90] *Ibid.*, p. 22, note 24. Document reference: AB. 9/64.

[91] Cited by Audrey Strange as *Transactions of the Leicestershire Archaeological and Historical Society*, Vol. 2 (1870), pp. 109-10 ('The Grey Friars, Leicester', *The Ricardian*, p. 5, note 10). Lankester's report is in *New Leicester Chronicle* 31 May 1862.

[92] Langley & Jones, *The King's Grave*, p. 15.

[93] Langley's list of burials produced for the Looking For Richard Project in 2011 (with later input by Ashdown-Hill, 2012).

[94] John Leland writing before 1543 says: 'The Greyfriars of Leicester stood at the end of Wigston's Hospital and there was buried King Richard III and a knight called 'Mutton', a one-time mayor of Leicester.' C.J. Billson believed that the tomb Leland noticed was that of 'Sir William Moton of Peckleton, Knight, who according to Burton was buried at the church of the Grey Friars in Leicester in 1362', Billson, *Mediaeval Leicester*, p. 79. Sir William Moton is also recorded as dying between 1356 and 1362, S.H. Skillington, *The Manor of Peckleton*, (1932), p. 103.

[95] Gilbert Luenor and his wife, Ellen were founders according to Stow: T. Tanner, *Notitia Monastica* (1744), p. 245, fn. 2.

[96] Said by Francis Peck to be a founder or early benefactor but no evidence supports this view, Nichols, *History and Antiquities of the County of Leicester*.

[97] Provincial Minister of Scotland, Vicar and Custodian of Oxford (c.1235). According to Leland's notes at Eccleston, Reresby died at Leicester; according to another account, he may have died at Acre in Norfolk: Andrew G. Little, *The Greyfriars in Oxford* (1892) p. 180 ch. III.

Leland when visiting recorded seeing two tombs: those of Richard III and a knight called 'Mutton' (Moton). Nichols recorded two further burials: 'Peter Swynerfled (Swynfeld), the 8th provincial of the Grey Friers [*sic*] in England, and William Nottingham, the 19th provincial'.[98] Thus, out of the eight possible burials, there were four potentially reliable names, of which only two might be considered certain.[99] Of these, only Richard III had been recorded as dying in battle.

By March 2011 Leicester City Council had agreed to facilitate the Looking For Richard Project, and the next step was for Langley formally to commission the local archaeological contractors ULAS to undertake a Desk-Based Assessment (DBA) to evaluate the archaeological potential of the Social Services site, including the adjacent New Street car park and that of the former grammar school. At a cost of £1,140, and funded via a bursary obtained by Langley on application to the Richard III Society, the DBA allowed ULAS, a firm of independent archaeological contractors whose offices were conveniently based at the University of Leicester campus, to commit its staff time to the project.

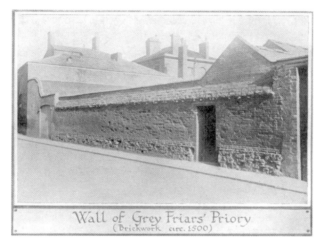

ULAS Report No 2011-038
©2011

Fig. 15: Front cover of the DBA Report with photograph showing the extensive mediaeval wall of the Franciscan Priory precinct (now demolished), taken looking south-east from Peacock Lane: the large building in the foreground is 'almost certainly' 16 New Street.[100]

---

[98] John Nichols, *History and Antiquities of the County of Leicester* (1795-1811), p. 297, note 18: *History of the Grey Friers* (London, 1726), part 2, p.12; J. Stevens, *The History of the antient abbey, monasteries, hospitals, cathedral and collegiate churches* (1722), vol. 1, p. 97. a.

[99] At the 2012 dig, one set of female remains was uncovered in a charnel burial within the choir of the church located in Trench Three in the former grammar school car park. A sarcophagus burial was also uncovered in Trench Three along with several grave cuts. In the dig undertaken in July 2013, the sarcophagus burial revealed a second set of female remains. It has been hypothesized that these may be those of Ellen Luenor, the only recorded female associated with the Greyfriars. In 2013, ULAS applied to exhume four graves uncovered during the first dig, including the sarcophagus burial.

[100] *An Archaeological Desk-Based Assessment for Land at Greyfriars, St Martin's, Leicester* (NGR: SK 585 043), Leon Hunt for: Philippa Langley, ULAS. Hunt was Site Supervisor at the subsequent 2012 dig.

44

But the agreement came with a caveat. ULAS agreed in principle to the commission subject to the reservation that they would not undertake it as a search for the grave of Richard III. They were, however, interested in excavating to see what could be discovered about the lost Greyfriars precinct and in particular the Franciscan Priory Church. Langley agreed to this on the basis that the project would nonetheless include provisions for the eventuality that human remains might be found in circumstances that could give reason to suppose they might be those of the king, and if so, they would be exhumed and DNA tests conducted.

Focusing on the history of the open car park areas, the DBA would use map regression analysis to document the land use over time. With the majority of sites in Leicester having seen significant disturbance from later buildings such as cellars, walls and service trenches, this would give the team an indication of the potential for any surviving archaeology. Langley submitted her research document to ULAS for the DBA and alerted them to the most recent publication of Ashdown-Hill's research in *The Last Days of Richard III*.[101]

Results were encouraging. The discovery of Thomas Roberts's map of 1741 was particularly interesting, as it showed an area which appeared to be Herrick's garden on the east of the site. Wendy Johnson suggested to Langley the possible significance of a central circular feature of the garden as the potential site of Herrick's pillar commemorating Richard III's grave. As a result, Langley asked ULAS to overlay a modern map of the Greyfriars precinct on to the formal garden area of the Roberts map (see Fig. 16).

Fig. 16: Thomas Roberts map of 1741 with overlay (2012) of modern road map (and trenches).

---

[101] '*The Greyfriars, Leicester*' consisted of a bullet-point reference document covering the main research topics conducted so far on Richard III's burial in the Greyfriars. Key among them was the most recent research by Dr John Ashdown-Hill (*Last Days of Richard III*, July 2010) refuting the 'bones in the river' story. It was important that ULAS understood there were sound historical reasons to disbelieve the tradition that the king's remains had been removed and destroyed.

This overlay showed that the central garden feature lay within the former grammar school car park and under the school building to the east. Assuming the map was accurate, if this central garden feature actually did hold the pillar which Herrick had inscribed 'Here lies the body of Richard III', it could mean that the grave lay under both tarmac and school. At this stage, however, it was all still speculative.[102]

The site of the car parks appeared to have remained in use as gardens from the time of the dissolution (1538) until the twentieth century when by 1944 the area came into use for vehicle parking.[103] At the same time, a bus depot had been built on the far western edge of the site at Southgates (see below). Furthermore, the DBA report added that: 'early descriptions of the site suggest the friary church … would have lain … opposite St Martin's church.'

Analysis of discoveries showed that most of the archaeological remains discovered on the western side of the site were Roman in date, suggesting moderate potential for remains of this antiquity to be discovered. Mediaeval remains included an Anglo Saxon urn found in the south-east in Friar Lane, with a possible mediaeval or post-mediaeval section of a wall of 'stone rubble and brick' located in the New Street car park. Stone footings representing an 'earlier stone cellar' were found at the rear of 12 New Street, with the nearby gardens revealing 'architectural fragments including tracery possibly of C14th date, possibly derived from the friary buildings'.[104] The photograph of the priory wall reproduced on the front cover of the DBA report was taken from Billson's *Mediaeval Leicester* (see Fig. 15 above).[105]

Although the Social Services car park and former grammar school remained largely undeveloped, map regression indicated an early twentieth-century garage or outbuilding in the north of the Social Services site and a library or book room farther east within the school area. Both seemed to have been single storey buildings with a footing/foundation depth of two to three feet. Impact on any potential archaeology was unclear. By 1955 these were no longer recorded and the library or book room was replaced by a bicycle shed (see Fig. 17).[106]

In terms of burials, the analysis confirmed a moderate potential in the car park areas based on previous discoveries during the eighteenth and nineteenth centuries when building work had taken place on the outer edges of the gardens[107] and around the postulated position of the church, with the former grammar school playground also having potential, being closer to the north-east corner of the Greyfriars precinct.

The DBA recommended: 'As a first stage, it is suggested that GPR survey could be tried within the Social Services car park with a view to picking up the principal walls of the church and perhaps claustral buildings. This could then be followed by a number of trial trenches to clarify the archaeological potential of the site and determine the position and projected plan of the principal buildings.'

By 2011 there was no further archaeological evidence at hand other than a watching brief on the demolition of the former bus depot in Southgates on the far west side. This location had

---

[102] During the 2012 dig, excavation in Trench Three (the school car park) uncovered what looked to be one of Herrick's garden paths running in a north-south direction, which seemed to suggest the garden was not located so far to the east; it could therefore encompass the king's grave, although not within the circular feature. [A second excavation (2013) may shed more light on the location and boundaries of the garden.]

[103] Detail of Goad insurance plan of 1944, Hunt, DBA (ULAS 2011) p. 14, figure 15. Buckley confirmed that the tarmacking of an area would generally act to preserve potential archaeology.

[104] *Ibid.* Hunt, DBA. Source: Derrick and Finn 2001.

[105] Billson (1920), 'Wall of Grey Friars' Priory' photograph by Newton, p. 140 (i).

[106] Christmas card of Alderman Newton's Boys' School, Leicester (1960) reproduced by courtesy of Dr Peter Foss.

[107] Georgian and Victorian buildings situated off St Martin's, Peacock Lane and New Street (replicating Throsby's account).

been assigned for redevelopment as an hotel, and enquiries with the local architect's office (Lee Staniforth) confirmed the majority of finds to be Roman pottery, with some mediaeval pottery. The main area to the south of the street frontages seemed to confirm map analysis, and suggested the area at mediaeval level was mainly gardens with 'horticulture or "backyard" activity'.[108] Langley had already planned for a GPR survey and cleared it with the council, so she now went ahead with commissioning this, raising the required finance (£5,043) from donors within the Richard III Society, members of the Scottish Branch and private investors.[109]

Fig. 17: Alderman Newton's Boys' School premises (1960).

With permissions received from the three landowners, a bank holiday weekend was chosen for the survey work. This would allow ease of access to the car park areas with the city council offices closed, while the former grammar school was already deserted and up for sale and redevelopment. The New Street car park would be surveyed first in the early morning in order to reduce any potential inconvenience to its permit holders. A privately-owned space and generally operated as a workplace facility, it would be closed for a couple of hours with holders forewarned.

[108] Albion Archaeology 2011: 'Former Bus Depot, Peacock Lane, Leicester. Archaeological Watching Brief and Field Evaluation. Project: Y.A6.2011. Document: 2011/114, 7th October 2011'.
[109] Appreciation to Dr Raymond Bord, David Fiddimore, Dr David and Wendy Johnson, Gerry Martin, Fiona Nicolson, Dr Phil Stone, Jack Thomson.

Stratascan, in Worcester, was commissioned to undertake the work. With many years' experience in urban surveying techniques and location studies of former church and burial sites, Stratascan would use the powerful MIRA scanner for the analysis.[110] The size of a small car (see Fig. 19 opposite) this would offer a good combination of penetration depth and resolution of the survey areas through its radar pulses at a mid-range frequency of 400MHz.[111] The extensive site of asphalt-covered car parks to be surveyed consisted of approximately 4,070 m^2 and would take a full day. Weather conditions were clear and sunny.

On Sunday 28 August 2011 the GPR survey of the three car park areas began. Its objective was to locate any anomalies that might be of archaeological significance but with particular reference to 'anomalies that may relate to a church that once existed in the area, along with any associated burials.' The Looking For Richard Project members were there to see it take place.

By 26 September 2011, Stratascan's report was complete.[112] Its results were inconclusive and alarming. A layer of apparent made ground or demolition debris near to the surface had affected the results. The survey had revealed a number of anomalies but most appeared to relate to surface features such as 'kerbs or inspection covers, or underground services such as pipes or cables'.

With no clear sign of coherent linear anomalies that could represent the foundations of the church or any former building, only on Langley's insistence could a potential grave site be cautiously postulated. This was in the former grammar school car park, represented by a small rectangular response in the centre (see area in red, Fig. 18).[113]

Fig. 18: Proposed locations of three trenches in relation to GPR results (WSI, July 2011).
The rectangular response area is circled, as is the 'Ruin' in the New Street car park.

---

[110] Appreciation to Claire Graham BA (Hons), Project Manager of Stratascan. Scanner supplied by LTU.
[111] The Mala GeoScience MIRA system collects sixteen channels of data at 0.08m centres, in swathes 1.28m wide.
[112] Geophysical Survey Report, Greyfriars Church, Leicester for Philippa Langley (September 2011) Ref. J2934, Robbie Austrums BSc (Hons).
[113] This rectangle response was the stone sarcophagus discovered at the 2012 dig.

Although the results were re-examined in more detail at Langley's request, the eventual conclusion was that it would take archaeological excavation to establish the true nature of the features identified, and trenching was recommended with targeted investigation of any anomalies of potential interest. Although disappointing, at least the survey results fully outlined the position of modern services which would aid ULAS's plan for the trenching work. Langley decided to proceed with the planning and costing of a three-week dig project.

In an attempt to pick up any potential east-west walls of the church (and/or claustral buildings), ULAS's trenches would run in a north-south direction. Trenches One and Two would be situated in the main target area of the Social Services car park as required by Langley, with the proposed adjacent Trench Three in the former grammar school area (see Fig. 18 above).

Langley had enquired about the possibility of test pits in case the locations decided by ULAS for the trenches missed certain key areas she wished to be explored; in the event, they were not required. Trench One would cover the northern end of the Social Services car park, the key research area for Langley and Ashdown-Hill. ULAS had mentioned they were aware that earlier excavation of the Austin Friars in Leicester had revealed the cloister garth to lie on the north side of the church. They said they were keeping an open mind, but felt that if this were to be replicated at the Greyfriars, then the church (and the king's grave) would be located in the heavily developed area to the south of the car park, and most likely beneath a building. However, they had not taken into account the vastly different layout and rural location of the Austin friars outside the city walls, as explained on pages 9–10 above, 'Mendicant Orders', and hence for Ashdown-Hill it was an unlikely model on which to base any expectations.

Fig. 19: MIRA scanner used for survey of car parks by Ground Penetrating Radar (2011).

The total costing from ULAS came out at £34,861 for the three-week project, the first two weeks being archaeology and the final week being allocated to restitution of the ground surface afterwards, the cost of which accounted for a sizeable element of the budget (see Appendix 3). By mid August Langley had secured all the necessary permissions from Leicester City Council, who agreed dates for her from 28 April to 20 May 2012. With ULAS requiring payment in advance, she would now enter a phase of intense fund-raising (see section 8, 'Facilitation').

The key document setting out the specification of work to be performed for the contractual fee was the Written Scheme of Investigation (WSI), the project plan required for all archaeological investigative work setting out the terms and conditions mutually agreed between the client (Langley) and contractor (ULAS).

This document constituted the sole legal instrument for Langley to place on record with ULAS, as recommended by the Ministry of Justice, those detailed provisions previously agreed as to the preservation of privacy, respect and dignity for the remains of Richard III should they be found.

With the entire framework for the project now in place, the one element that presented problems was the funding, discussed in the next section, 'Facilitation'. Owing to withdrawal of funds the budget could not be met in time for the reserved dates in April–May 2012, but fortunately the city council held open an alternative option in August the same year, by which date Langley managed to secure sufficient financing for the dig to go ahead.

The WSI now confirmed the details of the three-week archaeological evaluation project. Using trial trenching, the project would aim to provide preliminary indications for the preservation of archaeological remains associated with the Franciscan Priory Church. The investigation would offer four main archaeological objectives:

1. to identify the presence or absence of any archaeological deposits
2. to establish the character, extent and date range of any archaeological deposits
3. to identify any deposits relating to the priory church
4. to produce an archive and report of results

Two 30m trenches would be dug in the Social Services car park, followed by a third trench of up to 25m – this would be either in the former school playground or possibly in the same Social Services car park. The additional trench would aim to establish the presence of any burial, specifically that of Richard III. With time and budget constraints, any articulated human remains uncovered at the site would be left *in situ* and removed only if thought likely to be those of Richard III. In the event that remains likely to be those of the king were discovered they would, after specialist DNA, osteological and archaeological recording, be transferred to the custody of the client, Langley (or her representatives) for transfer to lie in a place of continual prayer and worship before eventual reburial.

8
Facilitation

Facilitating a project as ambitious as this archaeological search would be the key deciding factor in its accomplishment. Leicester City Council (owners of the Social Services car park) had been hit hard by the recession so the prospect of digging an important parking area that was constantly in use presented serious logistical difficulties. And although they would help facilitate the project if it became a reality (through their staff and processes), they would not be in a position to finance it. Philippa Langley set a tentative date of April 2012 in order to allow sufficient lead-time, and to attract the necessary financial backing.

Seeking a funding partner in such challenging circumstances meant that for the search project to have any hope of getting off the ground it required a powerful incentivizer: an enabler that would offer any funding partner a return for their investment even if the worst happened and nothing of significance was found at the dig. Television coverage, it seemed, could provide the answer.

Langley had already secured the rights to John Ashdown-Hill's book, *The Last Days of Richard III*, to protect against acquisitive TV producers. Her original three page proposal – with the working title *Looking For Richard: In Search of a King* – envisaged a documentary film with a unique blend of history, biography and archaeology, presented by a leading historian.

> '... *King Richard was laid to rest in the Franciscan Priory of the Greyfriars in Leicester. But with the dissolution of the monasteries, Richard's tomb was left to weather in its open ruins, his mausoleum taken and re-used, but leaving his mortal remains safe beneath the ground. This ground is thought to be the car park of the Social Services of Leicester and it is here that our search begins.*' (Looking For Richard: In Search of a King, 2010)

Julian Ware, Executive Producer of the award-winning Darlow Smithson Productions (*WW1: Finding the Lost Battalions*) was persuaded to commit his production company, and Channel 4 soon confirmed its interest in principle, which led to doors opening more readily than before. But there was one drawback: the broadcaster required something impossible to predict, namely a guaranteed on-screen result. The project had now secured a major funding partner, but they too sought a guaranteed return on investment. It was agreed to provide them with a short film for their website, to be aired in the event that the dig produced no results of historical interest.

A great deal now depended on the Ground Penetrating Radar survey, due to be conducted in August 2011 (see section 7 above, 'Local Topography and Archaeology'), which also heralded the start of filming by Darlow Smithson. Philippa Langley, John Ashdown-Hill, Annette Carson and the Richard III Society's Chairman Phil Stone were present to give short filmed interviews setting out the project's aims. It was hoped the forthcoming survey would reassure all stakeholders by revealing evidence of below-ground features that would encourage further examination. However, given its inauspicious results, understandably the projected financial backing was reconsidered. The original dig scheduled for April 2012 now had to be cancelled for lack of sufficient funding. Nevertheless, a reserve date of August 2012 was held open by the city council, so Langley began a new round of fund-raising. Among the contributions was a donation from the University of Leicester arranged by its Director of Corporate Affairs, Richard Taylor: he had in mind a video of the dig for their website. But still there was a huge and unsolved funding gap.

ULAS would not undertake work without money upfront in their bank account, so with Channel 4 still wary about the possibility that nothing worthwhile would be discovered, either a new, unconditional source of funding must be found to make up the shortfall or more than three years of effort faced abandonment. The Looking For Richard Project needed backing that was prepared to contribute money to the endeavour on its own merits.

Although independently conceived and actioned, this was a project that coincided with the founding principles of the Richard III Society: to promote research into the life and times of Richard III. By July 2012 the eleventh hour had been reached, and with three weeks to raise £10,000 the decision was made by Langley and Carson to mount a fund-raising effort hoping to tap into reserves of Ricardian generosity. Authorized by Chairman Phil Stone, a full-scale International Appeal was circulated by email to all branches, groups, members and supporters. Being such a speculative project, the full details had not hitherto reached the ears of members around the world: so it was Carson's task, as an experienced copywriter and communications professional, to produce a motivational presentation setting out the appeal with sufficient conviction to ensure an immediate response. An illustrated leaflet (see Appendix 7) was on its way within 48 hours, and the reaction was both positive and rapid, with pledges starting to arrive within minutes. The appeal raised well over the target figure, well within the target date.

It was now possible to embark on the three-week archaeological dig as planned, i.e. two weeks of excavation with a final week of work on re-installation and restoration. The new start date for the dig was 25 August 2012, and its new principal funding partners were the members and supporters of the Richard III Society as can be seen in the following figures. Appendix 3 shows the original breakdown of costs [£34,861.53] which was revised downwards (as below) following agreement by the University of Leicester to pay the coffin and pall costs should Richard be found, and pending final confirmation of alternative parking spaces required.

The team leading the project, although believing it had considerable historical significance, had little idea that it would become an international media phenomenon. With permissions and funding in place, the owners of cars graciously agreeing to park elsewhere, the archaeologists now paid and news cameras descending on the launch of the dig, Channel 4 officially commissioned the documentary. This last piece of the puzzle meant that all parties were irrevocably committed to the project's realization.

FUNDING RECEIVED FOR ARCHAEOLOGY COSTS, RICHARD III RETRIEVAL PROJECT

Richard III Society and members	17,367*	52.84%
University of Leicester	10,000	30.43%
Leicestershire Promotions Ltd	5,000	15.21%
Leicester Adult Schools	500	1.52%
Total:	£32,867	100

*Includes £100 donation from the Society of Friends of Richard III in York, and donations from some members of the Richard III Foundation Inc. Further funding of £716 from the International Appeal was paid to ULAS at the end of the dig for costs including the exhumation of Richard III. N.B. No part of this sum was used as compensation for travel, accommodation or any other personal expenses on the part of Philippa Langley (based in Scotland), John Ashdown-Hill (Essex), Annette Carson (Norfolk) or David and Wendy Johnson (Yorkshire), all of whom worked on the project entirely at their own expense.

9
The Dig

At a pre-dig meeting in Leicester on 6 August, the project's latest funding donor, the University of Leicester, requested and was granted the role of communications. With the chief facilitator in the enterprise, Leicester City Council, being over-stretched in manpower, and the university well versed in media output, it was an obvious fit. In preparation for the start of the dig on 25 August, 2012, the university placed at Philippa Langley's disposal their Press Office who would send out invitations to the project's media launch scheduled for Friday 24 August. They would also make a photographic and video record of the day's events. Aided by the skills of PR professional Annette Carson, an informative media pack was prepared and a press release distributed. Langley, Ashdown-Hill and Carson coped with most of the interviews, with Richard Buckley on hand to answer the myriad questions relating to the archaeology, while all the time emphasizing that ULAS regarded finding Richard III's grave as 'a long shot'.

In addition Langley had organized a number of distinguished visitors, including Dr Tobias Capwell, the Wallace Collection's Curator of Arms and Armour. The Chairman of the Richard III Society, Dr Phil Stone, who had been a donor and stalwart supporter of the project from its early days, sadly could not attend, being in Egypt at the time. The Mayor of Leicester was represented by the Assistant Mayor, Piara Singh-Clair; and Langley's principal liaison officer from the city council, Sarah Levitt, Head of Arts & Museums, was a welcome attendee. Richard Taylor from the university was invited, together with Dr Julian Boon, one of the UK's leading psychologists, who had agreed to talk to camera about his researches into the personality of Richard III. Michael Ibsen made the journey from London to be photographed as Dr Turi King took her DNA samples.

Television, radio and the press descended in droves, and most took advantage of photo opportunities provided by two splendidly accoutred re-enactors in authentic harness, Dominic Sewell and Henry Sherrey, who injected a flavour of the fifteenth century into an otherwise typically twenty-first century scene. Both gave their time on a purely voluntary basis, as did many others who wished to lend their support to the Looking For Richard Project. The media storm took Langley and her team by surprise, with the story appearing in news bulletins and press reports around the world as far away as India, Australia, Russia and Iran. That afternoon Channel 4 confirmed their decision to commission the film. From then onwards Darlow Smithson's cameras would be a constant presence.

Amid the heavy workload that preceded the launch, the trio of Langley, Ashdown-Hill and Carson scarcely had time to reflect on the fact that the official start of the excavation, Saturday 25 August, was the 527th anniversary of Richard III's interment in the choir of the Franciscan Priory Church.

The ULAS team had proposed two initial trenches in the Social Services car park, avoiding underground services and other features revealed by the Looking For Richard Project's GPR investigations. The mechanical excavator was brought in to dig the ground, operated with uncanny precision by its driver, Stevie Stell. ULAS Site Director was Mathew Morris.

By lunchtime the tarmac and soil had been dug to a depth of about two feet along a short stretch at the northern end of Trench One. This was the nearest excavation point to Langley's projected positioning of the king's burial and John Ashdown-Hill's projected site of the choir of the priory church.

At around ten minutes to three on Day One in Trench One with the trench depth at about 5 feet (about 1.5 metres) the driver was abruptly called upon to stop machining.[114] A length of human leg bone had been revealed, and it was important to ascertain whether this was part of a burial or a single, random find. The archaeologists, sceptical about the project's arguments as to the location of Richard III's grave, had been taken by surprise, not expecting to find human remains (or, indeed, signs of the precinct or church) at this point. The uncovered bone already showed signs of damage at some previous time in its history, so proceedings were halted while a little more soil was carefully removed by hand; this began to reveal a second leg bone lying alongside the first. Evidently this was part of an articulated skeleton, and work in that area now came to a halt because human remains could not be excavated without a Ministry of Justice exhumation licence. With the stratification levels yet to be determined there was no way to ascertain at present which century they belonged to, so they were to be left with a protective covering until more was known about the site and whether it would be right to exhume them. Langley, Ashdown-Hill and Carson realized that a great deal more digging had to be done to uncover evidence that would indicate if this area was indeed the priory church.

Over the ensuing week the necessary evidence came to light piece by piece, as fully reported in Langley's subsequent publication, *The King's Grave* (2013) co-written with Michael Jones. The archaeologists unearthed mediaeval floor tiles and remnants of a number of structures: gradually they built up a picture of features such as a cloister walk, the stone step of a doorway, and the stone bench of a chapter house. On Thursday 30 August in Trench One, only a few feet from the location of the lower leg bones discovered on the first day, the team uncovered the shadow of a massive wall, about five feet wide, which might be the wall of the church.

Friday 31 August marked the mid-way point of the two-week dig, and at a meeting between Langley (the client) and Buckley (lead archaeologist) it was agreed to cut the final trench – Trench Three – immediately adjacent to Trench One and farther to the east, in the car park of the former Leicester Grammar School which was separated from the Social Services car park by a sizeable Victorian brick wall running north-south. If the newly discovered evidence of the massive mediaeval wall proved to be that of the church, this would allow the team to pick up further signs of its continuation in the new trench.

Discussion now centred around the recovery of human remains. The agreed budget covering the work specified in the Written Scheme of Investigation (WSI) provided for one exhumation of human remains with full identification analysis. Buckley wanted to exhume in Trench Three, farther east, where he believed the east end of the church might lie. The remains in Trench One, in the archaeological team's estimation, would be too far west and therefore most likely those of a friar buried in the nave. Langley disagreed and pushed for exhumation of the remains already found in Trench One. Buckley informed her that extra funding would be required if this were to be done (to exhume these remains would also necessitate a small additional slot running west-east to be dug in order to gain access). Langley had nearly £800 left over from the International Appeal, which he confirmed would cover the extra charge.

The plan for the final phase of the dig was now in place. Early in the coming week, while work proceeded concurrently with Trench Three, the new slot would be dug over the remains preserved in Trench One. Buckley now left the site to fill in the Ministry of Justice application form for the exhumation licence back at his offices (see Appendix 6 below). ULAS had anticipated that Langley's budget would be sufficient to encompass up to six exhumations,

---

[114] The base of Richard III's grave was about 4ft 7in (*c*.1.4m) below present ground level.

therefore Buckley confirmed he would be applying to exhume up to six sets of unspecified remains. At this time, Darlow Smithson Productions applied to Langley to amend her agreement under the Written Scheme of Investigation (WSI) so as to permit a filmed record of the human remains. On the strict understanding that any filming would be for the historical record and not for wider dissemination, and would be kept securely by ULAS, Langley agreed to the amendment.[115] No other changes to the WSI were authorized.

That weekend, excavation of Trench Three in the school car park quickly yielded results. A pathway was uncovered that looked to be from Herrick's seventeenth-century garden, and the site of the church was indeed confirmed with the discovery of further enormous robbed walls, together with what looked to be a buttress on the northern side which faced St Martin's. Grave cuts were exposed, and by Monday 3 September the team confirmed with certainty that they had uncovered the priory church in Trench Three. Having achieved their objective, the attention of the archaeology team was now focused on the school car park, as further exploratory slots were dug to reveal more grave cuts and what looked to be the east end of the church.

Quietly, in Trench One, on the other side of the Victorian wall that separated it from the busy activity in Trench Three, exhumation of the human remains that were found on 25 August took place under the eye of Langley on 4 and 5 September. A male skeleton was uncovered with a clearly visible curvature of the spine and what looked to be severe battle trauma. Later that day (5 September), the archaeologists confirmed that the skeleton was located in the choir of the Franciscan Priory Church.

ULAS had reported to Langley that their unit's Senior Officer and Project Osteologist, Harriet Jacklyn (Lecturer in Human Osteology and Forensic Archaeology), was unavailable for this exhumation. This was a disappointment because Dr Jacklyn's considerable expertise with human remains had been intrinsic to the decision to place the commission with ULAS. Instead they brought in Jo Appleby, a young osteoarchaeologist who was Lecturer in Bioarchaeology at the University of Leicester with a principal interest in the Bronze Age. Working at the head of the body, Dr Appleby employed a mattock (a small pick-axe) to clear away the soil, having understandably estimated – by looking at the depth at which the legs lay in the trench – that the head would be lying at a similar depth. Instead, as it was later revealed, the position of the upper torso was at a higher level than estimated, and the mattock came into contact with the skull which was damaged as a consequence. The remains had otherwise survived in good condition since their owner was laid in the consecrated ground of the church 500 years previously, with the exception of the damaged leg-bones observed on the first day, and, as later reported in an article for the journal *Antiquity*, the absence of feet missing as a result of later disturbance, some of which was recorded to within 90mm of the lower limbs.[116]

Dr Turi King, who was present to participate in the exhumation as a trained archaeologist, ensured the area was treated as a 'clean-site', which entailed the wearing of protective masks and clothing to avoid any potential DNA contamination. Hence it was in an almost clinical atmosphere that the bones, which were later to be confirmed as the mortal remains of a King of England, were placed in a finds-box for safe removal from the site. As Ashdown-Hill held the box, Langley now placed over it the replica of Richard III's royal banner which he had brought to celebrate the launch of the dig and also in the hope that it might be put to this use. Ashdown-Hill then carefully carried the remains to the van that would take them away for DNA

---

[115] 11-177WSIGreyfriarsV_5: Clause 4.3.7: 'Furthermore, there will be filming of all human remains under investigation, but again the recotrd [sic] will be stored on a dedicated memory card and archived as above.'

[116] Missing skeletal remains from the exhumation included the left fibula, twelve hand bones (out of a total of fifty-four) both feet, and a few teeth. Langley & Jones, *The King's Grave,* Chapter 9 endnotes, p. 271.

identification. Extraction of ancient DNA would take a considerable time, but the agreement with ULAS provided for the identification process to be kept to the very minimum.[117] As noted above, should it transpire that the remains belonged to Richard III – not only a known individual with living relatives, but also an anointed king and former head of state – it had been mutually agreed that he would be treated with honour and respect, and his remains would be transferred without undue delay to an appropriate, prayerful environment to await reburial.

From the perspective of the historians and researchers who had pieced together the evidence that led them to invest in the project, there seemed grounds for considerable optimism as to the identity of the individual whose remains had been exhumed: he had a scoliosis, which accorded with the references to uneven shoulders that circulated after Richard III's death; he had battle injuries which were obvious at a glance; and his grave had been found, as predicted, in the choir of the Franciscan Priory Church, a prestigious area reserved for burials of the highest status. The team of Langley and Ashdown-Hill was joined at the site the next day by their colleagues Annette Carson and David and Wendy Johnson from the Looking For Richard Project, who arrived with innumerable questions about the discovery and its implications.

It had been agreed with ULAS that extreme caution must be exercised as to any disclosure before their process of identification had been completed – a process that was to be followed at every step by the documentary film cameras – while ensuring media excitement was firmly resisted until more was known. It was now Langley's responsibility to notify a very few people on a need-to-know basis. Using carefully chosen words, she called the office of HRH The Duke of Gloucester for whom she was the official point of contact for all the detailed preparations in the years leading up to the dig. A call was also made to Egypt to Dr Phil Stone, Chairman of the Richard III Society, whose members and other Ricardian supporters had become the majority funding partners in the dig. They had adopted the project wholeheartedly, and it was their generosity that made sure its endeavours did not fail.

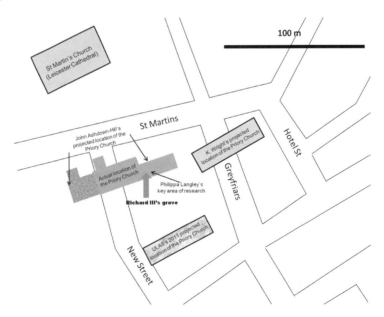

Fig. 20: Actual location of the Franciscan Priory Church compared to prior suggestions, with grave of Richard III indicated.

---

[117] The DNA matching, which was outsourced to the Universities of York and Toulouse, would normally have taken *circa* 4 weeks but in fact took *circa* 4 months owing to delays between the three universities.

10
Reburial and Commemoration

In February 2009, at the Cramond Inn near Edinburgh, Philippa Langley launched the search for the lost grave of Richard III (see above, page 36). The ethos of the Looking For Richard Project (LFR) was to ensure an honourable and dignified recovery and reburial of the king's mortal remains. It was therefore imperative that from the outset of the search these founding principles were established in all documentation before permissions were sought, and negotiations commenced, with relevant parties and organizations.

During the course of 2010 Langley commissioned David and Wendy Johnson, fellow members of LFR, to design a tomb for King Richard III which would be adopted as a formal proposal for his fitting commemoration. Accordingly the Johnsons began work on what became known as the Reburial Document, essentially a strategy document encapsulating the founding ethos of the project and outlining proposals for the recovery, reburial and commemoration of Richard's remains (see Appendix 1). At its heart was a detailed description and explanation of an entirely original tomb design, accompanied by sketches, line drawings, and in later versions of the document, a series of full colour Computer Generated Images (CGI).

The Reburial Document stated that 'As these are the remains of an anointed king the utmost respect must be maintained during the interval between discovery and reburial'. Therefore it incorporated details of Langley's provisions covering these concerns in her contract with ULAS, and agreed and endorsed by Leicester City Council. These set out controls on the way the remains would be treated, including the duration and purpose of scientific examination, restrictions on filming, photography and scanning, and arrangements for the spiritual preparation of the remains before reburial.

As well as details and illustrations of the tomb design itself, the Reburial Document also set out proposals for a coffin and a pall, a private reburial service, and a subsequent service of celebration at which the new tomb would be unveiled and blessed. The coffin was to consist of a simple box of English oak,[118] made with dovetail corner joints, large enough to hold Richard's skeleton in its anatomical position. The coffin would be lined with maroon coloured padding to cushion the remains and hold them in place (maroon being the closest approximation to murrey, one of the king's personal livery colours). A metal plaque, attached to the lid, and inscribed *Ricardus Rex Tertius*, would provide fitting identification. The pall was to be made of light beige damask like material, with a bright and shining gold cross at its centre, surrounded by a design of white, cream and matt gold flames representing the Holy Spirit.

It was suggested that the private reburial service should consist of either a mediaeval Vespers for the Dead or a mediaeval Funeral Mass, conducted in Latin, in accordance with Richard's Catholic religious beliefs. In June 2011 the Dean of Leicester Cathedral, the Very Revd Vivienne Faull, explained that this was broadly acceptable on the condition that required elements of the modern Anglican liturgy were included.

The centrepiece of the proposal was a detailed description and explanation of the research underpinning the tomb design. The Reburial Document developed and expanded as the design

---

[118] Following advice from Sarah Levitt at Leicester City Council, the wood was amended to elm.

of the tomb evolved and new drawings and images became available. Initially only pencil sketches and line drawings were featured, but by the early summer of 2011 these had been augmented with computer-aided design drawings by Simon Furniss. In July 2011 the Johnsons commissioned computer graphics specialists *Lost in Castles*[119] to produce a series of CGI images of the tomb. These were completed in time to be presented to the Dean of Leicester Cathedral on 28 August 2011. Over the winter of 2011/2012 details of the design continued to be refined and in late 2012, following discovery of Richard III's remains, the tomb was extended to include a plinth. In February 2013, after DNA identification of the remains was announced, the completed design was finally made public.

The tomb had taken more than two years to research and design, during which a number of challenges had to be addressed and overcome. First, there were the inescapable facts that this would be the second time Richard III had been buried, and that the two occasions were separated by more than five hundred years. So how could a new tomb reconcile the funerary requirements of a fifteenth-century English monarch with reburial in the twenty-first century? And second, there was the question of how the tomb design and inscription could reflect the history and identity of Richard III, a king who had, uniquely, forged strong ties with the north of England during his adult years as Duke of Gloucester and trusted lieutenant to his brother King Edward IV.

It was therefore proposed that the design should combine personally significant heraldic details with clean and relatively simple lines. There was no attempt to create a strictly traditional royal tomb as might have been expected for a King of England. The absence of a recumbent effigy, a common feature of mediaeval tombs, was intended to create a timeless monument conveying a sense of harmony and peaceful repose. And the unconventional inscription on the upper surface (see below) was intended to commemorate the entirety of Richard's life as well as his reign. In addition it was proposed that construction in Magnesian Limestone would represent Richard's important connections with Yorkshire and the City of York.[120] Its smooth, bright, honey-coloured appearance would symbolize Richard's transition from the darkness of his former resting place beneath a local authority car park to a more optimistic future in the light and spirituality of a religious space. Thus darkness to light became the overarching theme of the tomb.

The relative simplicity of the design was intended to reflect important surviving evidence concerning King Richard's personal religious preferences. His Book of Hours, dated to the 1420s, may have been as much as sixty years old by the time it came into his possession.[121] As a reigning monarch he could have commissioned the finest artists in Europe to illustrate a new and magnificent Book of Hours, yet he chose to use a second-hand volume lacking the lavish illuminations known to have been favoured by the courts of France and Burgundy.[122] As an example of the king's private and personal piety, this relatively modest and understated book can reasonably be assumed to reflect his wider religious tastes.

The proposed tomb was therefore similarly modest in scale and decoration, consisting of a plinth supporting a chest surmounted by a rectangular slab (length 7ft, width 3ft 6ins, height 2ft

---

[119] Grateful thanks to Joseph and Abigail Fox of *Lost in Castles*, www.lostincastles.com, whose skill and diligence repeatedly produced high quality images at short notice.

[120] York Minster was built of Magnesian Limestone, quarried locally from a site near Tadcaster south of York, and it is still used for repairs, maintenance and rebuilding.

[121] A. F. Sutton & L. Visser-Fuchs, *The Hours of Richard III* (1996), p. 39.

[122] For example, The Book of Hours of Marguerite de Foix, Duchess of Brittany, Rennes 1471-76, illustrated in R. Watson, *Illuminated Manuscripts and their Makers* (2003), p. 103. See also T. Tolley, *A Book of Hours* (1993): Plate 3, The Très Riches Heures of Jean, Duc de Berri illuminated by the Limbourg brothers *circa* 1435, and Plate 11, The Hours of the Duke of Bedford, Paris *circa* 1423, possibly a wedding gift from Bedford's brother-in-law the Duke of Burgundy.

3ins) (just over 2m x 1.5m x 0.69m). The initial design had been raised by the addition of a plinth following concerns over the low height of the original tomb chest. The intention was always to permit a comfortable appreciation of the inscribed upper surface of the memorial, hence the modest elevation of the overall tomb to approximately desk height.

The rectangular slab surmounting the chest had been carefully designed to incorporate three important features, each personally significant to the king. At the head, or what would be the west end of the slab, the Royal Coat of Arms of King Richard III was inlaid into the stone in gold coloured metal. The coat of arms depicted here was based on a drawing in Thomas Willement's *Regal Heraldry* of an illuminated initial letter taken from Richard's manuscript version of Vegetius' *De Re Militari* (On the Art of War) which, it has been suggested, was commissioned for Richard's son Edward of Middleham.[123] Beneath the coat of arms, in the lower half of the slab, in matching gold coloured metal, was an inlaid plaque inscribed in simple capital lettering:

RICHARD PLANTAGENET

1452 – 1485

DUKE OF GLOUCESTER

KING OF ENGLAND

And finally, at the foot of the slab, cut into the stone in unembellished capital lettering, would appear the personal motto with which Richard is indelibly associated:

LOYAULTE ME LIE

The significance of inscribing the king's motto directly into the stone was a vitally important part of the design – a physical representation of the fact that loyalty was deeply ingrained into Richard's personality and was an intrinsic part of his character. The plaque and motto were intentionally placed in close proximity, one above the other, following the example of Richard's signature with this motto as evidenced by a surviving document dated to May 1483.[124]

The careful positioning of the coat of arms, plaque and carved inscription was intended to leave an expanse of plain smooth stone, ensuring that the final effect would be one of proportion and harmony, designed to convey a sense of dignity, serenity, and elegant simplicity.

Similarly the side and end panels of the tomb chest were adorned with personally important commemorative imagery: a three-motif sequence consisting of a rose, a cross, and a boar. The

---

[123] P.W. Hammond & A.F. Sutton, *Richard III: The Road to Bosworth Field* (1985), p. 163; M.K. Jones, *Bosworth 1485: Psychology of a Battle* (2002), plate 12.
[124] BL Cott. MS Vespasian FXIII, f. 123; A. Carson, *Richard III: The Maligned King* (2008/9), p. 58; (2013), p. 67. Richard deliberately bracketed together his motto and signature, a possible indication of the importance he attached to the former.

first motif, the rose, depicts the badge of Richard's family, the house of York.[125] The mediaeval heraldic rose used here, consisting of an inner and outer circle of petals, is taken from Julian Rowe's illustration of King Richard's battle standard.[126] The white rose of York as used in the Middle Ages had various orientations, with the single point sometimes at the top (as in the rose in the arms of Edward IV's illegitimate daughter Isabella),[127] and sometimes at the bottom of the drawing. Examples of each can be found, and some where the rose has been given only four petals instead of five so that there is no top or bottom point.[128] Richard's standard as flown at the Bosworth Battlefield Centre on Ambion Hill has a white rose with the point uppermost.

The second motif, the cross, symbolizes the king's devotion to the Christian faith. The example represented here is based on the pectoral cross of St Cuthbert housed in Durham Cathedral. Richard's statutes bestowing collegiate status on the church of Middleham, in Wensleydale, demonstrate that he particularly venerated St Cuthbert.[129] Long before they were King and Queen, Richard as Duke of Gloucester and his wife, Duchess Anne Neville, were members of the fraternity of St Cuthbert which entitled them to celebrate mass in the choir of Durham Cathedral.[130]

The third motif, the boar, is Richard's personal heraldic emblem. The example depicted here is loosely based on a carved white boar taken from the pulpit of Fotheringhay Church in Northamptonshire, the family mausoleum of the house of York. Appropriately, the ornate pulpit was a gift to the church presented by Richard's elder brother, King Edward IV, in the mid-1470s.[131] The rampant posture of the heraldic beast is intended to represent Richard fighting back against the blackening of his character. And finally, the planned plinth upon which the tomb was to stand was adorned with capital lettering and two crosses:

+RICHARD III+

Richard's formal regnal number was given on both sides of the plinth so that the gold metal plaque on the surface of the tomb (described above) could stand as a more personal tribute.

Fig. 21: Details from the 'Looking For Richard' project's tomb design.
Images created by Joseph A. Fox, Lost In Castles, 2013.

---

[125] The rose was associated with the Virgin Mary and may have been adopted by the house of York for that reason.

[126] Hammond & Sutton, *The Road to Bosworth Field*, p. 216.

[127] H. Bedingfield & P. Gwynn-Jones, *Heraldry* (1993), p. 62.

[128] R. Marks & A. Payne, *Writhe's Garter Book*, p. 38.

[129] J.M. Melhuish, *The College of King Richard III Middleham* (issued by permission of the Richard III Society), p. 7. A stall in the collegiate foundation at Middleham was to be named after St Cuthbert, and the Saint's Day (20 March) was to be considered 'a principal fest'.

[130] A.J. Pollard, *Richard III and the Princes in the Tower* (1991), p. 76.

[131] Possibly on the occasion of the reburial of Richard Duke of York in July 1476. See J. Wilkinson, *Richard: The Young King To Be* (2008), plate 21; Jones, *Bosworth 1485*, plate 10.

Postscript

** On 5 September 2012, when the exhumed remains of Richard III were taken by ULAS for identification, they entered the premises of the University of Leicester. Although filming of Philippa Langley's Channel 4 documentary continued, from this point onwards the university took control of all media communications, as well as controlling which processes would be employed in examining the remains and who would be permitted access to them. At the date of this publication little more can be added in the way of certified information about the results, since Philippa Langley is still awaiting receipt of the formal report from ULAS. The firm's peer review process is understood to be still in preparation.

** In December 2012 a facial reconstruction was commissioned by the Richard III Society from Dr Caroline Wilkinson, Professor of Craniofacial Identification at the University of Dundee, based on the (as yet unidentified) human remains found in Trench One. When finished, Dr Wilkinson observed that the face bore a remarkable resemblance to portraits of Richard III, even though some had been painted a century after his death. The facial reconstruction was unveiled by the Richard III Society on 5 February 2013 and was exhibited during a tour of many major museums and historic sites with mediaeval associations.

** On 22 January 2013, Dr John Ashdown-Hill privately commissioned a funeral crown for Richard III's reburial. The idea for this had come to him in September 2012, when he carried the box containing the king's bones from the Greyfriars site, and he had subsequently put the plan to Philippa Langley and the Looking For Richard team. The design replicated the open style of crown that the king probably wore during the last days of his life, as he rode to the field of Bosworth at the head of his army on 21 August 1485, and over his helmet on 22 August, the day of the battle. A crown of this kind would have been a focal point in the king's funeral procession and burial had he been afforded royal obsequies in the fifteenth century. This crown, adorned with enamelled white roses (inspired by the surviving crown of Richard III's sister, Margaret, Duchess of Burgundy) and set with gemstones and pearls, is illustrated on the cover of this book.

** On the morning of 4 February 2013, the University of Leicester mounted a media event to announce that the mtDNA of the bones found at the Greyfriars site matched that of Richard III's living relatives. Dr John Ashdown-Hill, the discoverer of this mtDNA, was excluded from the announcement. The university's Professor of Greek Archaeology and History, Dr Lin Foxhall, who had played no part in the search or retrieval process, took the lead when it came to the historical background. Philippa Langley was allowed to give a short speech at the end after the media news feed was cut.

** On the evening of 4 February 2013 the documentary film made by Darlow Smithson Productions was transmitted by Channel 4 with the title *Richard III: the King in the Car Park*. It had been shortened from the original "Looking for Richard" concept as devised and developed by Philippa Langley (which had proposed a substantial historical research dimension), and now concentrated instead on the archaeological and scientific processes of August 2012–February 2013. The programme became Channel 4's highest rated specialist factual show in its thirty-year history. It won the 2013 Royal Television Society Award for Best History Programme and was nominated for a 2014 BAFTA in the category TV: Specialist Factual.

** On 13 March 2013 the project's tomb proposal – a design which had been welcomed by the Royal Household, and publicly endorsed by the Richard III Society whose members were the major funding partners – was ruled out by Leicester Cathedral. Initially it had indicated that the design would be part of the selection process. Instead the cathedral announced that 'the preference of Chapter, following informal consultation with the CFCE [Cathedrals Fabric Commission for England], is to mark the place of burial with a ledger stone'. Later, on 9 September 2013, responding to widespread concern about this plan, the cathedral produced a new and very modern tomb design. Meanwhile all the processes for the reburial and commemoration of Richard III previously agreed with Philippa Langley in the Reburial Document were set aside at this time, along with permission to allow the king's remains to be laid out in a prayerful environment to await reburial. It is hoped that these aspects will be reconsidered.

** In March 2013 Leicester's plans for Richard III's reburial in its cathedral were challenged by a group of his living relatives who had traced their collateral descent from the king and joined forces under the title of Plantagenet Alliance Ltd. A Judicial Review hearing was granted in the High Court of Justice, Queen's Bench Division, which was heard in two sittings on 26 November 2013 and 13–14 March 2014. The judgment, delivered on 23 May 2014, stated 'there are no public law grounds for the Court interfering with the decisions in question'.

Appendix 1

The Reburial Document (introductory pages)

Looking For Richard: In Search of a King

The Discovery and Reburial of King Richard III

As its title suggests, the thrust of the proposed archaeological living history special TV programme, '*Looking For Richard: In Search of a King*' is the story of THE SEARCH (to find King Richard III). Its success, therefore, is not based, or dependent upon, actually finding him. The search itself is the story. The fact of the mere 'looking for Richard' and the journey that this will take its audience on will produce a wholly captivating and unprecedented programme.

However, for the programme (and search) to begin it is of course understood and acknowledged that it can only go ahead on the basis and expectation of finding King Richard, together with all the necessary permissions in place that this will require.

A Royal Burial

Richard III was an anointed king. He is also an ancestor of the Queen. It is therefore important to state clearly, here, at the outset within this document what the programme's intentions are, and must be, with regard to the potential discovery of any remains.

If Richard's remains are found, they will be treated as a royal burial. Therefore:

- The remains to be allowed the <u>minimum</u> period required for scientific analysis for the purposes of identification <u>only</u>.
- For this to take place in the specialist unit in Leicester University.
- No filming / photography and / or visual record to be made of any kind of the remains, and / or placed on any record.
- When identification is complete, for Richard's remains to be taken directly to the cathedral, church, or other secure holy place in Leicester, to await reburial.
- Any other remains found at this time to be accorded the same.

It is a requirement of this programme that there must be no disturbance of the remains other than that required for identification purposes. Anything that may be construed as upsetting to descendants to be wholly contrary to the programme's focus and, therefore, unacceptable.

These basic principles are to ensure not only the honouring of Richard III's remains as an anointed king with living descendants, but also to impress upon the programme's audience the stature of the city that holds these remains. This is in accordance with the most recent programming in this field. Notably, '*WW1: Finding the Lost Battalions*' (Channel 4, July 2010).

Discovery

It must be remembered that in 1485 King Richard's remains were accorded a Christian burial and that they have lain in what was (originally) consecrated ground ever since. Thus it is important to ensure that the period of exhumation is kept to a minimum and King Richard's remains returned to a sacred environment as soon as possible.

The site of the Social Services car park in Leicester is a secure, enclosed area (walled, gated, and monitored by CCTV) of approx. one-third of an acre.

On the discovery of any grave and/or human remains, a gazebo-like covering shall protect the area from any high-level visual intrusion i.e. from any nearby windows etc.

At this time all filming will be from a LATERAL perspective only i.e. across the dig. No filming and / or visual record to be made of the grave and / or human remains at any time.

Full Christian rites are to be said over the grave(s) before removal / disinterment.

The site cleared, and remains covered and enclosed, before PRIVATE disinterment.

Secure transportation of the remains to the specialised unit at Leicester University.

Recovery

The recovery of any human remains in and around Leicester City Council's Social Services car park area will enable identification by DNA analysis to commence. Great care should be taken to ensure that the DNA process does not exceed one month. Work of this kind generally takes one to two weeks to generate a result.

As these are the remains of an anointed king the utmost respect must be maintained during the interval between discovery and reburial. Therefore the remains should not be subjected to any form of photography, scanning, or filming whatsoever. Due reverence must be observed at all times and any form of disturbance avoided as a matter of priority.

Following positive identification, and until reburial can take place, the remains should be cared for in a quiet, safe, holy place. Here, in accordance with the rites and rituals of Richard's own time, spiritual preparation for burial could be observed in surroundings of continual worship and prayer.

Appendix 2

Richard III's Tomb – the Epitaph

Dr John Ashdown-Hill's important research on Richard III's epitaph was originally published in 2008.[132] For many years the epitaph had been neglected, and doubts cast on its authenticity. Subsequently, his original conclusions relating to the meaning of the main line of received text (Wriothesley-Hawling-Sandford) have been slightly updated as a result of discussion with Dr Emily Keans, whose views on the epitaph are due to be published shortly in *The Ricardian*.

Evidence relating to the date of the Epitaph

At least two manuscript copies of the epitaph are extant and were rediscovered by Ashdown-Hill. The earlier of these, BL Add. MS 45131, f. 10v, is from the collection of Sir Thomas Wriothesley (d. 1534), and is probably in his handwriting.[133] Thomas Wriothesley was one of the sons of John Wrythe,[134] a herald during the reigns of Edward IV, Richard III and Henry VII. Wriothesley was a pursuivant in the private service of Arthur Tudor, Prince of Wales (1489), and he was later (1503) Garter King of Arms.[135] At the time of Thomas Wriothesley heralds kept their own libraries and BL Add MS 45131 is a compilation comprising some of Wriothesley's personal reference material.

The inclusion of a copy of Richard's epitaph in this collection securely dates its composition before 1534. Indeed, its context within the collection suggests a date prior to 1531, and it could well be earlier.[136] Wriothesley's copy of the epitaph was therefore written before the 'Dissolution of the Monasteries', at a time when Richard III's tomb in Leicester was still extant and undamaged. At this period heralds' visitations were beginning to take place, and while no record of a visit by Thomas Wriothesley to Leicester survives, such a visit, either by Thomas himself or by one of his colleagues, is possible. Thus BL Add. MS 45131, f. 10v may be a copy taken directly from an inscription on or by Richard III's tomb. The fact that the writer changed his mind about some of the readings suggests that he might have been working directly from such an inscription.[137]

Sandford's manuscript source for his 1677 published text of the epitaph was the second of the extant manuscript copies: College of Arms MS I 3, f. 4.[138] This copy, clearly derived from the Wriothesley text, is in the handwriting of Thomas Hawley, who became a herald in 1509 and died in 1557.

---

[132] 'The Epitaph of King Richard III', *The Ricardian* Vol. XVIII, 2008, pp. 31-45. See also Ashdown-Hill *Last Days of Richard III* (2010), pp. 100-103, 135-7; (2013), pp. 101-105, 164-5; and plates 26, 27.

[133] 'My opinion is that this is indeed the handwriting of Sir Thomas Wriothesley, or if not his own is the same as a contemporary hand to be found in manuscripts compiled by or associated with him'. Personal communication from Mr Robert Yorke, Archivist at the College of Arms, December 2006. Appreciation to Mr Yorke for his opinion on this point.

[134] Thomas changed the family surname.

[135] Biographical details relating to Thomas Wriothesley and his father from the *ODNB*, from *College of Arms: Collections*, vol. 1, p. 502 (unpublished) and from A.R. Wagner, *The Records and Collections of the College of Arms* (1951), p. 9.

[136] In the same gathering as the epitaph there is a text referring to an anniversary mass for Louise of Savoy, Regent of France, celebrated at Waltham Abbey in 1531.

[137] For Wriothesley's manuscript text (which differs a little from Sandford's wording) see below.

[138] Appreciation to Richmond Herald (Mr P.L. Dickinson) for this information, and to Mr Robert Yorke, Archivist of the College of Arms, for his extensive help during examination of this manuscript.

Sir George Buck's published text appears to belong to a separate line of transmission, distinct from the Wriothesley–Hawley–Sandford tradition. Buck reported his source for the epitaph as a text at the Guildhall, stating that in or shortly before 1619 a book which contained the relevant folio was 'chained to a table in a chamber in the Guildhall of London'.[139] Buck's Guildhall source cannot have been identical with Sandford's source at the College of Arms.[140] Apart from any other consideration, differences in the two texts rule this out. The Guildhall copy of the epitaph has not been traced, and is probably not extant.

Thomas Wriothesley's MS text:
BL Add. MS 45131 f. 10v (old enumeration, p. 20), c.1495-1534.

       Epitaphe   Ricardi R/ 3[ij] [141]

Hic ecco aîo[142] qζ vano[143] tellus sub marmore claudit
tercius multa voce Ricardus eram
nam[144] patris tutor patrius[145] pro iure nepot[an *erased*][146]
dirupta tenui Regna Bretanna fide
Sexaginta dies binis dûtaxat a[b *erased*]demptis   5
Estates qζ tuli non[147] mea Sceptra duas
fortiter in bello merito desertus ab anglis
Rex henrice tibi septim[is *erased*][148] succubui
at sumptu pius ipê tuo sic ossa decoras
Non[149] Regem facis Rege honore Coli   10
quatuor exceptis iâ tûcû[150] quinqζ bis annis
acta trecenta quidê lustra salutis erant
ante qζ Septembris undena luce Kalendas
Reddideram Rubre debita Iura Rose
Set att[151] mea, quisquis eris ρ'pter cõmissa ρ'care   15
Sit minor ut precibus pena forenda[152] tuis

---

[139] *The History of King Richard the Third by Sir George Buck,* ed. A.N. Kincaid (1979), p. 217.

[140] F. Sandford, *A Genealogical History of the Kings of England* (London, 1677), p. 410.

[141] The words *Ricardi Regis 3[ij]* have been added in a later hand.

[142] Abbreviation for *animo*? That word, however, makes no sense in this context, and produces too many syllables for the scansion.

[143] Or *vario* - both make sense.

[144] The original reading may have been: *Nam patriae tutor patrius pro jure nepotum'*.

[145] Perhaps an error for *patruus*?

[146] An abbreviation for *nepotum* (nephews, in the plural)? Both Buck and Sandford use the singular noun *nepotis*.

[147] *non mea* = 'not mine'.

[148] The transcriber seems to have been uncertain how to complete this word, which was probably abbreviated.

[149] This line as it stands does not scan properly in either manuscript.

[150] This is probably a misreading of *tâtû* (abbreviation for *tantum*).

[151] Perhaps an error for *Sed ac*, but the scansion is wrong.

[152] Perhaps an error for *ferenda* (= 'must be borne'). This would not greatly alter the essential meaning of the line. Scansion does not help here in choosing between the various readings, since *levata, fienda* and *forenda* (for which read probably *ferenda*) all scan the same.

Translation of Sandford's published text of 1677

I, here, whom the earth encloses under various coloured marble,
Was called by many 'Richard the Third'.
I was Protector of my country, an uncle ruling on behalf of his nephew.
I held the British kingdoms by broken faith.
For sixty days less two,   5
And two summers, I held sceptres which were not mine.
Fighting bravely in war, deserted by the English,
I succumbed to you, King Henry VII.
But you yourself, piously, at your expense, thus honour my bones
And you cause a former king to be revered with the honour of a king.   10
Subtract fourteen,
From the three hundred five-year periods of our salvation which had passed,[153]
And eleven days before the Kalends of September
I restored to the red rose the rights it had lost.
Whoever you are, pray for my offences,   15
That my punishment may be lessened by your prayers.

---

[153] According to this reading the author had miscalculated, producing a year date of 1486 when he meant 1485.

Appendix 3

Archaeological Dig Costs Breakdown
(Final, September 2011)

GREYFRIARS, LEICESTER
A: Archaeological Costs (Excl. VAT)

Tasks	Post	day rate	days/units	Total
1. Preparation of WSI etc	Director	£300.00	2	£600.00
2. Site setup/preliminaries	Site director	£263.98	1.5	£395.97
3. Week 1 machining/excavation	Site Director	£263.98	5	£1,319.90
	Site supervisor	£250.00	5	£1,250.00
	Site assistant 1	£242.90	3	£728.70
	Site assistant 2	£242.90	3	£728.70
4. Week 2 Investigation	Site Director	£263.98	5	£1,319.90
	Site supervisor	£250.00	5	£1,250.00
	Site assistant 1	£242.90	5	£1,214.50
	Site assistant 2	£242.90	5	£1,214.50
			TOTAL	**£10,022.17**
5. Contingency overtime				
Four 2hr Evenings	Site Director	£263.98	1	£263.98
	Site supervisor	£250.00	1	£250.00
	Site assistant 1	£242.90	1	£242.90
	Site assistant 2	£242.90	1	£242.90
			TOTAL	**£999.78**
Saturday	Site Director	£263.98	1.5	£395.97
	Site supervisor	£250.00	1.5	£375.00
	Site assistant 1	£242.90	1.5	£364.35
	Site assistant 2	£242.90	1.5	£364.35
Sunday	Site Director	£263.98	2	£527.96
	Site supervisor	£250.00	2	£500.00
	Site assistant 1	£242.90	2	£485.80
	Site assistant 2	£242.90	2	£485.80
			TOTAL	**£3,499.23**

6. Machining costs (excl. VAT)	Excavation	£250.00	3	750.00
	Roading in/out			300.00
	Contingency exc.	250	1	250.00
			TOTAL	**1,300.00**
7. Post-Excavation Analysis (excl. VAT)	Site Director	£263.98	10	2,639.80
	Finds specialists	£263.98	2	527.96
	Finds processing	£242.90	1	242.90
			TOTAL	**3,410.66**
			GRAND TOTAL	**£19,231.84**

B: Other Costs (excl. VAT)				
1.Alternative car parking	(57x£3.50x15)			**£2,992.50**
2. Commissionaire				**£750.00**
3. Night security	£863.52 per 7 days	£863.72	2	**£1,727.44**
4. Tarmac/compaction£40 sqm	£41.15sqm (City Highways)	£41.15	205	**£8,435.75**
5. Relining	£210 EST			**£210**
			TOTAL	**£14,115.69**
			GRAND TOTAL	**£33,347.53**
C: Reburial costs				
Coffin (incl. VAT)				£1,164.00
Pall (incl. VAT)				£350.00
			PROJECT TOTAL	**£34,861.53**

Suggested initial trench locations in relation to two possible layouts for church and claustral ranges.

Fig. 22: Two possible layouts for the Greyfriars priory produced with initial costings in April 2011 by ULAS at the request of Langley showing potential sites for the church in the Social Services car park. Note that both plans place the church considerably too far south.

Appendix 4

Leicester City Council Permissions
Looking For Richard Project

Please ask for: Alistair Reid
Direct Line: 0116 252 7352
Email: Alistair.Reid@leicester.gov.uk
Date: 12 August 2011

Leicester
City Council

Philippa Langley
Little Marilyn Productions
40 Charlotte Square
Edinburgh
EH1 4HQ

Dear Philippa,

Re: Project proposal: Looking for Richard: In Search of a King" (working title) hereinafter referred to as "the Project"

Thank you very much for your proposal and all the detailed development work you have put in to it. We are now in a position to respond formally.

To: Philippa J. Langley, her partners and/or successors, hereinafter known as "the Client":

1. We hereby give permission for the Client to carry out a GPR survey of the Social Services Car Park at Greyfriars provided that:

1. There is no direct cost to Leicester City Council.

2. This permission is a permission to undertake a GPR survey only, no other access and no connections are included.

3. This permission does not extend to the rights and property of third parties, or any other permissions or consents that may be required.

4. No other activities are involved (except as referred to Clause 2 below).

5. Leicester City Council Property Services, Adults and Community Services and Children's and Young People's Services are happy with the arrangements the Client agrees with them. (Contact Mick Bowers, Resources Support Manager, to confirm this). This is now confirmed with Mick Bowers, Resources Support Manager who is happy with the arrangements the Client has made with them.

6. The area to be surveyed is to be indicated on a plan agreed in advance by Mick Bowers. Only the area shown in the plan will be subject to survey. Plan is submitted and agreed with Mick Bowers.

7. There is no physical disturbance of Leicester City Council property and the Client leaves the site in the same condition as the Client found it.

8. Whilst we will use our best endeavours to ensure that cars, skips and other temporary items are cleared, the Client accepts that this may not be practicable in all cases and that the Council is not obliged to incur any cost. If this happens we will let the client know in as far as possible in advance.

REGENERATION, CULTURE AND DEVELOPMENT
Block B, New Walk Centre, Welford Place, Leicester LE1 6ZG
TELEPHONE:(0116) 252 7352 www.leicester.gov.uk

71

9. The Client agrees that none of the proposed activities creates a relationship of employment, principal or agent or partnership between the Client and Leicester City Council.

10. The Client provides satisfactory details in advance of public and third party insurance.

11. The GPR Survey takes place on Sunday 28th August 2011. If it is not completed within the agreed weekend the Client must apply for further permission to complete the survey.

12. Permission given for the GPR survey does not imply permission is given by Leicester City Council for any future investigations.

13. Full copies of all reports with recommendations are provided to Leicester City Council.

14. Any press releases and media communications are agreed with us in advance.

15. Leicester City Council shall appoint a contact for the Client, and shall provide the Client with contact details, who is to be made available at the Social Services car park on Sunday August 28th 2011 from 08.45 – 17.00 hours. This is to ensure that the car park is opened for the Client at 08.45, for the GPR survey to take place, and thereafter for the car park to be secured. A mobile number for the contact shall be given to the client before Sunday 28th August 2011, in order to ensure the above takes place as stated. Should the contact be unable to attend the social services car park in Greyfriars on the stated day and times, another shall be appointed by LCC as a matter of urgency, in order to ensure that the Social Services car Park on Grey Friars is opened to allow the GPR survey to take place, and secured at the end of the survey. The lead officer for ensuring this happens is Mick Bowers.

2. We hereby give permission for the client, and any other individuals or organisations contracted by the client and for whom the Client provides details to us in advance, to make or commission a film in the Social Services car park at Greyfriars, in relation to the Project and we will waive our normal film location charges provided that:

1. There is no direct cost to Leicester City Council

2. The producer of the film (or his/her delegated officer) on behalf of the film company obtains filming location permission in advance. (This should be arranged via Maggie Shutt, Festivals and Events ManagerTel:0116 238 5081 Maggie.Shutt@leicester.gov.uk).

3. We agree in advance the dates that filming is to take place in the Social Services car park at Greyfriars. Any further filming will need separate permission from us.

4. This permission only relates to the Social Services car park at Greyfriars.

5. This permission does not extend to the rights and property of third parties, or any other permissions or consents that may be required.

6. This permission is related to the GPR survey only, no other access and no connections are included.

2

7. There is no physical disturbance of Leicester City Council property and the Client leaves the site in the same condition as the Client found it, and clears away all rubbish and equipment.

8. There is no catering on site and no permission is given to use toilet or catering facilities inside the Greyfriars building.

9. The Client will indemnify us in writing against all claims, costs proceedings etc relating to rights of, or permissions required by, third parties, arising out of the activity and the content of the film and any associated publication or media content.

10. The Client agrees that none of the proposed activity creates a relationship of employment, principal or agent or partnership between the Client and Leicester City Council.

11. No other activities are involved (except as referred to in Clause 1 above).

12. This is for the purpose of producing a documentary film intended for broadcasting.

13. Leicester City Council's assistance should be acknowledged in any broadcast, publicity, advertising, book publishing, merchandise, exhibitions or other works (Works) and in any and all media (whether now known or hereafter invented) throughout the world.

14. The Client provides satisfactory details in advance of public liability insurance.

15. The Client agrees in advance any reasonable requirements for business continuity and anonymity relating to council officers, cars or office locations with Mick Bowers since this is a sensitive work location.

16. A copy of any finished film of broadcast quality is provided to LCC on DVD together with permission for LCC and Leicestershire Promotions limited to use it free of charge for promotional purposes after the date of the first UK screening by a broadcaster, or as otherwise agreed with the Client.

3. We hereby give permission for a further archaeological investigation in connection with the Project, the biography and presence of King Richard III in Leicester, and the making and broadcasting of the film of any excavation in the Social Services car park at Greyfriars, on substantially the same terms, and we will waive our normal film location charges provided that:

1. The provisional date of Saturday 28 April – Sunday 20 May 2012 is confirmed and agreed in advance with Mick Bowers, Resources Support Manager.

2. There is no direct cost to Leicester City Council.

3. The Client submits a project description, scheme of investigation, impact assessment and health and safety plan, and these are satisfactory to us. These are now confirmed with Chris Wardle, City Archaeologist for Leicester City Council, who is happy with the 'Scheme of Work' as provided by the Client and the University of Leicester Archaeological Services (ULAS).

4. We are satisfied that funds are secure to complete the work properly and make good.

3

5. Standard conditions/professional practices relating to the archaeological archive, including all finds, fossils, antiquities and human remains will be applied to any permission. All such material remains in the ownership of and is the responsibility of Leicester City Council during and after excavation.

6. Apart from in relation to (5.) above, no permission will be granted to film actual human remains at any time whatsoever during the course of the Project. (Please refer to Leicester Museums' human remains policy on the council's web site for further details regarding the respectful treatment of human remains). Please also refer to clauses 4.2.8 and 4.3.7 in the 'Scheme of Work'.

7. Furthermore any photography or photographic record made of remains identified beyond the balance of probability as those of King Richard III, for whatever purpose, are to be allowed only, and as stated, in the 'Scheme of Work', specifically clauses 4.3.5 and 4.3.6 and will only take place following consultation with Philippa J Langley.

8. Philippa J Langley, as the nominated point of contact for the Duke of Gloucester, will be at liberty to verify the application of the above clauses 6 and 7 during the entire course of the Project.

Please note also that if any further projects or activities are proposed which relate to human remains excavated in Leicester at any time these will need to be the subject of a separate discussion and further approvals.

Please contact Sarah Levitt, Head of Arts and Museums, if you require any further assistance, and to provide details of permissions, insurances etc. as set out above.

Yours sincerely

Alistair Reid
Strategic Director
Development, Culture and Regeneration
Leicester City Council

4

Appendix 5

The Written Scheme of Investigation (WSI)
(pages recording the clauses agreed with ULAS, as amended)

UNIVERSITY OF LEICESTER ARCHAEOLOGICAL SERVICES

Written Scheme of Investigation for Archaeological Investigation

Job title: Social Services Car Park, Greyfriars, Leicester

NGR: **SK 585 043**

Client: Philippa Langley and /or her nominated partner / successor (hereinafter referred to as 'the Client')

1. Introduction

1.1 *Definition and scope of the specification*

This document is a design specification for an archaeological investigation via trial trenching at the above site. The fieldwork specified below is intended to provide preliminary indications of the potential for the preservation of archaeological remains associated with the Greyfriars friary church, which once occupied the site.

1.2 The archaeological investigation will take the form of an archaeological field evaluation, which according to the Institute for Archaeologists Standards and Guidance: for Archaeological Field Evaluation (2008) is a limited programme of non-intrusive and/ or intrusive fieldwork which determines the presence or absence of archaeological features, structures, deposits, artefacts or ecofacts within a specified area or site on land, inter-tidal zone or underwater. If such archaeological remains are present field evaluation defines their character, extent, quality and preservation, and enables an assessment of their worth in a local, regional, national or international context as appropriate.

2. Background

2.1 Context of the Project

2.1.1 The Client has been granted permission by Leicester City Council to use archaeological methodology to attempt to locate the remains of the Greyfriars friary church, which stood on the site at Greyfriars during the medieval period and is believed to be the final resting place of Richard III, the last of the Plantagenet kings, who was killed on Bosworth Field in 1485.

2.1.2 In consultation with University of Leicester Archaeological Services (ULAS), the programme of archaeological work is to commence with Ground Probing Radar Survey followed by trial trench investigations to locate any archaeological remains associated with the Greyfriars buildings. A further trench will then be examined to locate the choir, the presumed burial place of Richard III.

2.2 Archaeological and Historical Background

Text condensed from Desk Based Assessment of the site (Hunt 2011)

2.2.1 The site lies within the walls of the Roman town of Ratae Corieltavorum (HER Ref: MLC72) and within the walls of the subsequent medieval town. Several known Romano-British remains are known from the Greyfriars site as a whole and from the close vicinity. These include three tessellated floors (MLC235, MLC236 & MLC1209) and part of a Roman building (MLC352).

2.2.2 The Priory of the Grey Friars in Leicester is said to have been founded in 1255 by Simon de Montfort, who was the Earl of Leicester from 1238-1265. The buildings were said to extend from the upper end of the Market Place to the Friar Lane meeting house and lay opposite St. Martin's church.

2.2.3 Richard III (2 October 1452 – 22 August 1485) was King of England for two years and was the last king of the House of York and the last of the Plantagenet dynasty. After the death of Edward IV in April 1483, Richard was named Protector until the young Edward V became old enough to rule in his own right. When the children of Edward IV were declared illegitimate Richard, as next in line to the throne, accepted the crown.

2.2.4   Two major rebellions against his reign led to the Battle of Bosworth Field in 1485, where the armies of the House of York met those of the Lancastrians under Henry Tudor. Richard was killed on the battlefield and his body was returned to Leicester. The Grey Friars of Leicester either requested or were charged with the disposal of his remains and contemporary reports confirm that the body was buried two days after death within the Friary. One witness John Rous gives the choir as the place of burial (Baldwin 1986). Evidence from around 1495 reports that Richard's tomb had an alabaster cover.

2.2.5   The church of the Grey Friars was destroyed in 1538 shortly after the Dissolution of the Monasteries. The popular account is that Richard's body was removed from the coffin, carried through the city by jeering crowds and cast into the River Soar at Bow Bridge, or buried nearby the bridge. There are, however, no contemporary reports to confirm that this actually took place.

2.2.6   A house later occupied the site and accounts suggest that during this and later development various human remains were unearthed. There is tradition that Richard's tomb was reused as a drinking trough for a local public house but there is no evidence that the tomb was ever removed from its original site.

3.   Archaeological Objectives

3.1   The main objectives of the investigation will be:
*   To identify the presence/absence of any archaeological deposits.
*   To establish the character, extent and date range for any archaeological deposits
*   To identify any deposits relating to the Friary church
*   To produce an archive and report of any results.

3.2   Trial trenching is an intrusive form of archaeological investigation that will demonstrate the existence of earth-fast archaeological features that may exist within the area.

4.   Methodology

4.1   *General Methodology and Standards*

4.1.1   All work will follow the Institute for Archaeologists (IfA) Code of Conduct (2010) and adhere to their *Standard and Guidance for Archaeological Field Evaluation* (2008). The LCC *Guidelines and Procedures for Archaeological work Leicestershire and Rutland* (1997) will be adhered to.

4.1.2   Staffing, recording systems, health and safety provisions and insurance details are included below.

4.1.3   Internal monitoring procedures will be undertaken including visits to the site by the project manager. These will ensure that project targets are met and professional standards are maintained. Provision will be made for external monitoring meetings with the Planning Authority and the Client, if required.

4.2   *Trial Trenching Methodology*

4.2.1   Prior to any machining of trial trenches general photographs of the site areas may be taken.

4.2.2   A CAT scanner will be passed over the proposed trenching area to locate any unknown services.

4.2.3   A Ground Probing Radar Survey has been undertaken (Fig 1) revealing a number of potential archaeological anomalies and areas of what may be spreads of rubble, although it has not proved possible to positively identify Friary structures to inform the precise location of trial trenches. In view of this, two trenches measuring 30m x 1.6m will be placed within the Social Services Car Park area, oriented north-south, located to avoid services known from maps and the GPR survey. The long length and orientation of the trenches will give a greater likelihood of exposing archaeology given that the position of the building is unknown and the basic layout of a church and claustral buildings would mean many walls running east- west across the site.

4.2.4   An additional trench of up to 25 square metres will be investigated with a view to establishing whether any burials are present, specifically those of Richard III. This may either be in the adjacent Wyggeston School Car park or in the Social Services car park.

4.2.5   Measured drawings of all archaeological features will be prepared at a scale of 1:20 and tied into an overall site plan. All plans will be tied into the Ordnance Survey National Grid. Relative spot heights will be taken as appropriate.

4.2.6   Sections of any excavated archaeological features will be drawn at an appropriate scale. At least one longitudinal face of each trench will be recorded. All sections will be levelled and tied to the Ordnance Survey Datum, or a permanent fixed benchmark.

4.2.7   Trench locations will be recorded by an appropriate method. These will then be tied in to the Ordnance Survey National Grid.

4.2.8   Any articulated human remains encountered will initially be left in situ and will only be removed if thought likely to be those of Richard III, under Ministry of Justice guidelines and in compliance with relevant environmental health regulations.   Excavation of such remains shall be carried out with due care and attention, shielded from the public gaze (using CSI tenting) including any potential high-level visual intrusion from neighbouring windows and rooftops, with recording as specified below, see particularly 4.3.5 & 4.3.6 in relation to photography. In order to prevent cross contamination of samples for DNA testing, staff will ensure that suitable protective clothing is worn (gloves, masks, lab coats) during the excavation of articulated human remains.

4.2.9   Upon completion, the trenches will be backfilled and consolidated to highways specification and re-tarmaced. The Social Services car park will be swept clean and any white lines will be reinstated.

4.2.10   The Social Services car park gates will be secured for the duration of the works and individual trenches enclosed with orange plastic barrier fencing.

4.2.11   Leicester City Council will ensure that the Social Services car park is made clear of all public vehicles and / or potential obstructions (skips etc) on, and by, the evening before the works begin. ULAS shall install Heras fencing as indicated on Fig 1 and access will be possible for Social Services staff to parking spaces on the western and southern sides of the car park via the New Street and Greyfriars gates respectively. Each of these entrances will become two-way and it is understood that Leicester City Council will put measures in place to ensure the safe operation of these points of access and egress. It is estimated that approximately 37 spaces will be affected by the excavation of the initial two trial trenches; depending on the location of the contingency trench, further spaces could be affected for the second week. During the time of the works there will be no public access to the Social Services car park site unless previously agreed with the Client. This does not include any access required by, or on behalf of the Client for the purposes of filming.

4.2.12   Night security will be employed (from 8pm to 8am) in order to protect the site. This will begin as soon as the trenches are cut (estimated as Saturday 25th August 2012) and continue for approximately two weeks (14 nights) thereafter until either: the trenches are backfilled, and / or it is confirmed by ULAS that there are no archaeological remains on site (human and / or otherwise). Night security to be supplied by Chris Allman, Head of Security at Leicester City Council Social Services who has quoted £10.28 per hour for a security officer (£123.36 per night shift). See archaeological costings below.

4.3   *Recording Systems*

4.3.1   Any archaeological deposits encountered will be recorded and excavated using standard procedures as outlined in the ULAS recording manual. Sufficient of any archaeological features or deposits will be hand excavated in order to provide the information required.

4.3.2.   Individual descriptions of all archaeological strata and features excavated or exposed will be entered onto prepared pro-forma recording sheets.

4.3.3   A record of the full extent in plan of all archaeological deposits encountered will be made on drawing film, related to the OS grid and at a scale of 1:10 or 1:20. Elevations and sections of individual layers of features should be drawn where possible. The OD height of all principal strata and features will be calculated and indicated on the appropriate plans.

4.3.4   An adequate photographic record of the investigations will be prepared illustrating in both detail and general context the principal features and finds discovered. The photographic record will also include 'working shots' to illustrate more generally the nature of the archaeological operation mounted.

4.3.5   Each individual burial will be photographed using standard silver-halide film and individual still photographs will be carefully numbered and logged at the time they are taken, with one film used per burial. At this time, all photographs of human remains will be processed by ULAS and kept in a secured location at the University. In accordance with the wishes of the Client, digital photography will be allowed in relation to human remains exposed during the course of the investigation, but all images will be stored on a dedicated memory card.. Special provision will be made for the archiving of photographs of any human remains which have been positively identified as those of Richard III (see below: 4.3.6)

4.3.6 The film (negative) and the photograph (positive), together with memory card containing digital photographs of the remains positively identified as Richard III will be kept together in a secured archive. Only those persons from the recognised scientific community and with reasons of substantiated legitimate scientific research will be allowed, by the authority of Leicester City Council Arts & Museums Services, appropriate access to view the photographic record of the remains. That apart, strictly no photographic equipment of any kind (mobile phones, cameras etc) will be allowed into the secure area during the time of viewing of the photographic record of the remains. The control of the photographic record, as detailed above, will be subject to legal enforcement by Leicester City Council Arts & Museums Services, should this be required.

4.3.7 Furthermore, there will be filming of all human remains under investigation, but again the recotrd will be stored on a dedicated memory card and archived as above.

4.3.8 This record will be compiled and fully checked by ULAS and the Client during the course of the project.

5. Finds

5.1 The IfA *Guidelines for Finds Work* will be adhered to.

5.2 Before commencing work on the site, a Site code/Accession number will be agreed with the Leicester City Museums Service and used to identify all records and finds from the site.

5.3 All antiquities, valuables, objects or remains of archaeological interest, other than articles declared by Coroner's Inquest to be subject to the Treasure Act, discovered in or under the Site during the carrying out of the project by ULAS or during works carried out on the Site by the Client shall be deemed to be the property of ULAS provided that ULAS after due examination of the said Archaeological Discoveries shall transfer ownership of all Archaeological Discoveries (excluding any human remains identified to be those of Richard III) unconditionally to Leicester City Museums Service for storage in perpetuity.

5.4 All identified finds and artefacts are to be retained, although certain classes of building material will, in some circumstances, be discarded after recording with the approval of the City Archaeologist.

5.5 All finds and samples will be treated in a proper manner. Where appropriate they will be cleaned, marked and receive remedial conservation in accordance with recognised best practice. This will include the site code number, finds number and context number. Bulk finds will be bagged in clear self sealing plastic bags, again marked with site code, finds and context.

5.6 Finds which may constitute 'treasure' under the Treasure Act, 1996 must be removed to a safe place authorised by ULAS and reported to the local Coroner and to the Client. Where removal cannot take place on the same working day as discovery, suitable security as determined by ULAS will be taken to protect the finds from theft.

5.7 Any human remains which are positively identified as those of Richard III will, after specialist DNA, osteological and archaeological recording, be transferred to the custody of the Client and/or the Client's representatives for reburial. At this time, the remains will be placed in a hand-made coffin (provided by the Client, please see Client's 'Reburialv2' Document). It is then proposed that the remains will be transferred to the nearby Abbey of Mount St. Bernard (provided suitable security can be guaranteed) where they will lay in a place of continual prayer and worship before private reburial in Leicester Cathedral. Such private reburial will not, under any circumstances, be filmed or photographed at any time. At a later date, the private reburial will be followed by a 'Celebration Ceremony' and unveiling of a new tomb. However, the 'Celebration Ceremony' will be available to be filmed and / or photographed as required. Please see the Client's 'Reburial Documentv2' as agreed with Leicester Cathedral.

6.   **Environmental Sampling**

6.1.   If features are appropriate for environmental sampling a strategy and methodology will be developed on site following advice from ULAS's Environmental Specialist.   Preparation, taking, processing and assessment of environmental samples will be in accordance with current best practice. The sampling strategy is likely to include the following:

- A range of features to represent all feature types, areas and phases will be selected on a judgmental basis. The criteria for selection will be that deposits are datable, well sealed and with little intrusive or residual material.

- Any buried soils or well-sealed deposits with concentrations of carbonised material present will be intensively sampled taking a known proportion of the deposit.

- Spot samples will be taken where concentrations of environmental remains are located.

- Waterlogged remains, if present, will be sampled for pollen, plant macrofossils, insect remains and radiocarbon dating provided that they are uncontaminated.

6.2   All collected samples will be labelled with context and sequential sample numbers.

6.3   Appropriate contexts (i.e datable) will be bulk sampled (50 litres or the whole context depending on size) for the recovery of carbonised plant remains and insects.

6.4   Recovery of small animal bones, bird bone and large molluscs will normally be achieved through processing other bulk samples or 50 litre samples may be taken specifically to sample particularly rich deposits.

6.5   Wet sieving with flotation will be carried out using a York Archaeological Trust sieving tank with a 0.5mm mesh and a 0.3mm flotation sieve. The small size mesh will be used initially as flotation of plant remains may be incomplete and some may remain in the residue. The residue > 0.5mm from the tank will be separated into coarse fractions of over 4mm and fine fractions of > 0.5-4mm. The coarse fractions will be sorted for finds. The fine fractions and flots will be evaluated and prioritised; only those with remains apparent will be sorted. The prioritised flots will not be sorted until the analysis stage when phasing information is available. Flots will be scanned and plant remains from selected contexts will be identified and further sampling, sieving and sorting targeted towards higher potential deposits.

6.6   Where evidence of industrial processes are present (eg indicated by the presence of slag or hearth bases), samples will be taken for the analysis of industrial residues (e.g hammer scale).

7   **Report and Archive**

7.1   A draft version of the report will normally be presented to the Client and the Local Planning Authority within four weeks of completion of site works. The full report in A4 format will usually follow within eight weeks. Copies will be provided for the Client and the Local Planning Authority and deposited with the Historic Environment Record (HER).

7.2   The report will include consideration of:

- The aims and methods adopted in the course of the evaluation.

- The nature, location and extent of any structural, artefactual and environmental material uncovered.

- The anticipated degree of survival of archaeological deposits.

- The anticipated archaeological impact of the current proposals.

- Appropriate illustrative material including maps, plans, sections, drawings and photographs (excluding any photographs in relation to the remains of Richard III as defined in clauses: 4.3.5 & 4.3.6 as above).

- Summary.

- a summary of artefacts, specialist reports and a consideration of the evidence within its local, regional, national context.

- The location and size of the archive.

- A quantitative and qualitative assessment of the potential of the archive for further analysis leading to full publication, following guidelines laid down in *Management of Archaeological Projects* (English Heritage).

7.3 A full copy of the archive as defined in the IfA Standard and Guidance for archaeological archives (Brown 2008) will normally be presented to Leicester City Museum Service within six months of the completion of fieldwork. This archive will include all written, drawn and photographic records relating directly to the investigations undertaken and will follow the LCC guidelines detailed in *The Transfer of Archaeological Archives to Leicester City Museums Service* (LCMS) 2006.

7.4 The copyright of all original finished documents shall remain vested in ULAS and ULAS will be entitled as of right to publish any material in any form produced as a result of its investigations however with the exception of any photographic material in relation to the remains of Richard III as defined in clauses: 4.3.5 & 4.3.6 as above.

8 Publication and Dissemination of Results

8.1 A summary report, as approved by the Client, will be submitted to a suitable regional archaeological journal following completion of the fieldwork. The full report, as referred to in 7.1 above, will be submitted to a national or period journal if the results are of significance.

8.2 University of Leicester Archaeological Services supports the Online Access to the Index of Archaeological Investigations (OASIS) project. The online OASIS form at http://www.oasis.ac.uk will be completed detailing the results of the project. ULAS will contact the HER prior to completion of the form. Once the report has become a public document following its incorporation into the HER it may be placed on the web-site. This will not, however, include any of the photographic record of the remains, or any part of the remains, identified as those of Richard III as defined in clauses: 4.3.5 & 4.3.6 as above.

8.3 Any such publication will be in accordance with clause 10.2 below.

9 Acknowledgement and Publicity

9.1 ULAS shall acknowledge the contribution of the Client in any displays, broadcasts or publications relating to the site or in which the report may be included.

9.2 ULAS and the Client shall each ensure that a senior employee shall be responsible for dealing with any enquiries received from press, television and any other broadcasting media and / or members of the public. All enquiries made to ULAS shall be directed to the Client.

10 Copyright

10.1 The copyright of all original finished documents shall remain vested in ULAS and ULAS will be entitled as of right to publish any material in any form produced as a result of its investigations.

10.2 Publication of its investigations, in the first instance, shall be referred to the Client for agreement. This is to ensure that all publication by ULAS will occur only after the UK broadcast of the programme(s) has first taken place.

11 Monitoring arrangements

11.1 Unlimited access to monitor the project will be available to both the Client and their representatives and Planning Archaeologist subject to the Health and Safety requirements of the site.

11.2 All monitoring shall be carried out in accordance with the IfA *Standard and Guidance for Archaeological Field Evaluations* (2008)

11.3 Internal monitoring will be carried out by the ULAS project manager.

12 Timetable and Staffing

80

12.1 The work is to begin with machining of the initial two trenches on Saturday 25 August 2012. The work is likely to take 14 days to complete and up to four experienced archaeologists will be present during the work, together with up to three volunteers.

12.2 The on-site director/supervisor will carry out the post-excavation work, with time allocated within the costing of the project for analysis of any artefacts found on the site by the relevant in-house specialists at ULAS.

12.3 If human remains are identified as potentially belonging to Richard III, best endeavours are to be made to ensure a minimum period for the laboratory identification work, including the DNA investigation.

13 Health and Safety

13.1 ULAS is covered by and adheres to the University of Leicester Statement of Safety Policy and uses the ULAS Health and Safety Manual (revised 2010) with appropriate risks assessments for all archaeological work. A draft Health and Safety statement for this project is in the Appendix. The relevant Health and Safety Executive guidelines will be adhered to as appropriate.

14. Insurance

14.1 All ULAS work is covered by the University of Leicester's Public Liability and Professional Indemnity Insurance. Public Liability Insurance and Employers Liability Insurance: Allianz Insurance plc Policy No. SZ/21696148. Professional Indemnity Insurance – Novae Underwriting Ltd. Policy No. 702610MMA120

15. Contingencies and unforeseen circumstances

15.1 In the event that unforeseen archaeological discoveries are made during the project, ULAS shall inform the site agent/project manager, Client and the Planning Archaeologist and Planning Authority and prepare a short written statement with plan detailing the archaeological evidence. Following assessment of the archaeological remains by the Planning Archaeologist, ULAS shall, if required, implement an amended scheme of investigation on behalf of the client as appropriate.

16. Bibliography

Baldwin, D.. 1986. King Richard's Grave in Leicester. *Transactions of the Leicestershire Archaeological and Historical Society* Vol 60, p21-24

Brown, D., 2008   *Standard and guidance for the preparation of Archaeological Archives* (Institute for Archaeologists)

IfA, 2008   *Codes of Conduct and Standards and Guidance for Archaeological Field Evaluation.*

Hunt, L *An archaeological desk-based assessment for land at Greyfriars, St. Martin's, Leicester* (SK 585 043). ULAS Report No. 2011-038

Leon Hunt/Richard Buckley
ULAS
University of Leicester
University Road
Leicester LE1 7RH

Tel:0116 252 2848
Fax: 0116 252 2614

Email: rjb16@le.ac.uk

© 19 July 2012

Appendix 6

The Exhumation Application and Licence

**Application form for authority to exhume buried human remains
for archaeological purposes**

Please answer all questions.

Section 1: Applicant details

Name	Richard Buckley	Phone number	0116 2522848/0776 2546960
Address	University of Leicester	Email address	rjb16@le.ac.uk
	Archaeological Services		
	University Rd., Leicester	Fax number	0116 2522614
Post Code	LE1 7RH		

Section 2: Site details

Name (if any)

Address   1-7 Grey Friars/4-8 St Martins
(car parks to rear of)
Leicester

Post Code   LE1 5PH

Is the site consecrated according to the rites of the Church of England?   Yes [ ]   No [X]

Is the site owned by any church or religious organisation?   Yes [ ]   No [X]

If 'Yes', by whom? [ ]

Is the site a burial ground (please tick A, B or C below)

A	in use?		B	disused?		C	no longer a burial ground?	X

If the site is no longer a burial ground, please provide brief details of its history and current use?

The site is believed to be that of a Franciscan Friary, dissolved in 1538 and demolished shortly afterwards. It is now occupied by offices of the social services department, Leicester City Council, housed in a variety of buildings of the 18th-20th centuries which surround a central car park, and by a former School between 4 and 6 St Martins (see attached plan).

Has the site been (please tick A, B, C or D below)

A	cleared of human remains?		B	built over?	X
C	put to agricultural use?		D	returned to countryside?	

Has the site been acquired (please tick A, B or C below)

A	commercially?		B	by compulsory purchase order?		C	Act of Parliament?	

NOT APPLICABLE

Section 3: Human remains

Estimated age of remains	Medieval 13th-16th century	(if not all of the same date, please indicate range)
Estimated number of set of remains	6	
Estimated by	Richard Buckley	
Qualification	BA FSA MIFA, Director of ULAS	

Please provide details of what is being undertaken at the site and for what purpose the remains are to be excavated.

A research excavation is underway to investigate the remains of Leicester's Franciscan Friary and also potentially locate the burial place of Richard III whose remains were interred here in 1485, although these may subsequently have been exhumed and thrown into the nearby River Soar after the Dissolution in 1538. It is proposed to exhume up to six sets of human remains for scientific examination.

Are trial pits / trenches intended *(for site investigations)*? Yes [X] No [ ]

Section 4: Archaeological Project details

Start date	25.8.2012
Completion date	21.9.2012

Please indicate whether the remains are to be (please tick A, B, C or D below)

A	reinterred	B	cremated	C	left in situ	D	WISH TO RETAIN [X]
							Please note: in the unlikely event that the remains of Richard III are located, the intention is for these to be reinterred at St Martins Cathedral. Leicester within 4 weeks of exhumation.

Please provide location details of the final destination of remains and estimated date

Location LAURA HADLAND (Curator)
JEWRY WALL MUSEUM
ST NICHOLAS CIRCLE

Address	
	LEICESTER

Post Code	LE1 4LB

estimated date	JULY 2014

Section 5: Public health details

Please provide the name and address of the Environmental Health Officer for the site

Name	Tony Farrant
Address	Leicester City Council, New Walk Centre, Welford Place, Leicester

Post Code	LE1 6ZG

Email:	coroners@justice.gsi.gov.uk.
Fax:	0203 334 2233
Post:	Coroners Unit, Burials Team, Ministry of Justice, 102 Petty France, London SW1H 9AJ

The Exhumation Licence

LICENCE FOR THE REMOVAL OF HUMAN REMAINS

The Secretary of State, in exercise of the power vested in him by section 25 of the Burial Act 1857 (20 & 21 Vic., cap.81), grants a licence for the removal of the remains of **persons unknown** from or within the place in which they are now interred at **1-7 Grey Friars/ 4-8 St Martins (car parks to rear only), Leicester, LE1 5PH.**

2. It is a condition of this licence that the following precautions shall be observed:

    (a)   Any removal or disturbance of the remains shall be effected with due care and attention to decency;

    (b)   The ground in which the remains are interred shall be screened from the public gaze while the work is in progress;

    (c)   The remains shall, no later than 31 August 2014, be deposited at Jewry Wall Museum or else be reinterred at St Martins Cathedral or in a burial ground in which interments may legally take place. In the meantime shall be kept safely, privately and decently by the University of Leicester, Archaeological Services under the control of a competent member of staff.

3. This licence merely exempts those from the penalties, which would be incurred if the removal took place without a licence. It does not in any way alter civil rights. It does not confer the right to bury the remains in any place where such right does not already exist.

4. This licence expires on **31 December 2012**.

Rekha Gohil
on behalf of the Secretary of State for Justice

Ministry of Justice
Licence Number: **12-0159**

File Number: **OPR/072/91**
Date: **3 September 2012**

RICHARD III URGENT ARCHAEOLOGY APPEAL

An appeal in aid of the archaeological search for the lost grave of King Richard III – to raise £10,000

An urgent appeal for Ricardians and their friends to band together and make it possible for this once-in-a-lifetime excavation to take place in the city of Leicester, where the body of Richard III was buried after the battle of Bosworth.

In late August 2012 archaeologists are due to excavate the site which, after exhaustive investigations, is believed to be his most likely last resting place, in the Choir of the former Church of the Greyfriars.

New map regression analysis and Ground Penetrating Radar have helped to pinpoint the location, and it is here that the first-ever search for the grave of an anointed King of England will begin.

Detail from a map of Greyfriars, Leicester (1741)

Facilitated by Leicester City Council, and in association with the Richard III Society, the project is funded by prestigious local organisations including the University of Leicester, whose experts will be on hand to examine any discoveries and conduct DNA analysis if appropriate.

In short, everything is on schedule and ready to get under way . . . except that a sudden and unexpected shortfall of £10,000 has been encountered. The lack of this sum, although it represents only a proportion of the overall budget, will mean abandonment of the project.

This appeal is intended to make good the deficit and ensure the dig goes ahead as planned.

At the moment we are seeking pledges only, NOT money. All sums are welcome, whether large or small.

But the closing date is very soon. Please note that we need to receive all pledges by Friday 20 July, 2012.

On the next page are full details of how to make your pledge and how funds will be handled.

The aim is to film the dig, and negotiations are in place for a potential landmark TV special – not only documenting the archaeology, but also bringing the story of the **real** Richard to our screens for the very first time, with input from specialists including Dr John Ashdown-Hill and Annette Carson.

Leicester's Greyfriars Project Roll of Honour

Beds & Bucks Group of the Richard III Society
Gloucester Branch of the Richard III Society
East Midlands Branch of the Richard III Society
Lincolnshire Branch of the Richard III Society
(Former) Mid-Anglia Group of the Richard III Society
New England Chapter of the Richard III Society, USA
New Zealand Branch of the Richard III Society
Norfolk Branch of the Richard III Society
North Mercia Group of the Richard III Society
Northwest Chapter of the Richard III Society (US Branch)
Notts & Derby Group of the Richard III Society
Richard III Society of Canada
Scottish Branch of the Richard III Society
St. Swithun's Society, Canada
Sussex Group of the Richard III Society
Thames Valley Branch of the Richard III Society
The Society of Friends of King Richard III, UK
Victoria Branch of the Richard III Society, Australia
West Surrey Group of the Richard III Society
Worcester Branch of the Richard III Society

Stuart Akers, UK
Grant Alexander, UK
Dr John Ashdown-Hill, Turkey
Anne Ayres, UK
Sally Badders, USA
Norma Bassett, Canada
Gail Beardall, UK
Margaret Bentley, UK
Pam Benstead, UK
Lorelie Bond, USA
Helen Brickell, UK
Angela Brown, UK
Carole A. Brown, USA
Tracy Bryce, Canada
Debora Carr, USA
Lillian Carr, New Zealand
Sybil Carter, UK
Annette Carson, UK

Dr Tim Carter, UK
Mary Cheyne, USA
Alison Clark, UK
Alison Coates, UK
Anthony C Collins, USA
Cris Reay Connor, UK
Helen Corkin, USA
Jacqueline C. Cox, USA
Julia Cranston, UK
Florence (Babs) Creamer, UK
Iris Day, UK
Barbara Gaskill Denvill, Australia
Rita Diefenhardt-Schmitt, Germany
Mark Dobson, UK
Roger & Linda Dowlen, UK
Linda Drew, UK
Jean Edwards, UK
Leonid Elbert, Canada
Jacqui Emerson, UK
Elizabeth York Enstam, USA
Stephanie Bronder Fagan, USA
John C Farrell, USA
Gilda Felt, USA
Jean Fitzpatrick, UK
Donna Flatley, USA
Garry Fletcher, UK
Kate Fletcher, UK
Jane Forsyth, UK
Mary Friend, UK
Katheryn Gallant, USA
Judy Gardner, USA
Pamela Garrett, UK
Roswitha Gerhart, Germany
Linda Gilliland, UK
Hannelore Gormley, UK
Bethan Groom, UK
Brenda Groves, UK
Aubrey Gunn, UK
Elizabeth (Liz) Hamilton, UK
Joanna Hamminga, Holland
Muhammad Hanif, Turkey
Sandra Hardy, UK
Paul Harper, Canada
Jonathan Hayes, USA
Maureen Heal, UK
Sally Henshaw, UK
Jean Hester, UK
Patricia Hibbs, UK
Diane Hoffman, USA
Christine Holmes, UK
Lisa Holt-Jones, Canada
Vicki Horwood, UK
Sue Howlett, UK
Eleanor E. Huebner, UK
Karen Huisman, USA
Elaine Hunt, UK
April Hussong, USA

Wayne Ingalls, USA
Judith Anne Jackson, UK
Susan Jeeves, UK
David & Wendy Johnson, UK
Pat & Mike Joseph, UK
Mary Kelly, UK
Sally Kiel, USA
Joann Koch, USA
Karen (Kaye) Ladniuk, Brazil
George Langley, UK
John Langley, UK
Marigold Langley, UK
Philippa Langley, UK
Eileen T. Lehner, USA
Mark Lewis, UK
Dr Martin Litherland, UK
Clive Lloyd, UK
Bob Long, UK
Yvonne Mary Love, UK
Ken & Mary Lowles, UK
Joan B. Mach, USA
Donald MacLachlan, USA
Judith Fitzgerald Madore, Canada
Renate Maria Maier, Germany
Margaret Manning, NZ
Garry Marnoch, Canada
Sandra Martenson, USA
Gerry Martin, UK
Isolde Martyn, Australia
Victoria (Vicki) Mather, UK
Muriel Ann McDonald, UK
Geraldine McDonnell, UK
Farrah McFadden, Canada
Sofia Meaden, UK
Dr Liselotte Messner, Austria
Mhora Millar, UK
Chris Mitchell, UK
Anabel Morris, UK
Nancy Mosley,USA
Marion Moulton, UK
Shah Mugaseth, UK
Nita Musgrave, USA
Right Rev'd George Nairn-Briggs, UK
William Narey, USA
Kristen Negrotto-Weber, USA
Jane Nixon, UK
Helen O'Dea, Australia
Janet Oliver, UK
Bettina Ortiz, USA
Caroline (Callie) Kendall Orsak, USA
Micki Parkinson, USA
Pat Parminter, UK
Patricia Payne, UK
Dianne Penn, UK
Alfred (Dave) Perry, UK
Jerilyn Peterson, USA

Eva Pitter, Austria
Carolyn Preston, USA
John Priestley, UK
Patricia Pugh, USA
Patricia Pullen, UK
Ben Ravilious, UK
Charles Rees, UK
Vivian Reeves, UK
Ralph Richardson, UK
Joan Ripley, UK
Julie Roberts, UK
Elizabeth Robinson, UK
Starla Roels, USA
Ian Rogers, UK
Janet Rose, UK
Lesley A. Scott, UK
Neville Sibery, UK
Katherine (Kitty) B Simmons, UK
Jane Skelton, UK
Rose Skuse, UK
Rob Smith, New Zealand
Anne Easter Smith, USA
Niz Smith, UK
Simon Smith, UK
Isobel Sneesby, UK
Elizabeth Sommers, USA
Fletcher Stewart, Canada
Lilian Stockton, UK
Christine A. Stone, UK
Dr Phil Stone, UK
Georgina Ann Strachan, UK
Pamela Strong, UK
Ruth Stroud, UK
Gayna Stuart, UK
Joan Szechtman, USA
Judy Gerard Thomson
Diana Thompson,
Traxy Thornfield, UK
Nikoletta Toth, Hungary
Mollie Toy, UK
David Wilfred Turner, UK
Annamarie Vallis, USA
Richard Van Allen, UK
Erika Van de Sande, Belgium
John & Joyce Varty, UK
Bob Vivian, USA
Brian Wainwright, UK
Diana Wallis Dornella, UK
Cynthia Waterman, UK
Doug Weeks, UK
Sue & Dave Wells, UK
Rosemary (Rosie) Anne Wileman, UK
Elaine Williams, UK
Linda Williams, USA
Doug Woodger, Canada
Ann Wroe, UK
Nessa Wyberd, UK

Grateful thanks to all who contributed and helped to make history

Bibliography

van Alsinghen, J.F. Gislenus Cuypers, *Provincie, Stad, Ende District Van Mechelen*, Vol. 2 (Jorez, Brussel, 1770)

Ashdown-Hill, J., *The Last Days of Richard III* (Stroud, 2010, 2013)

Ashdown-Hill, J., *Richard III's Beloved Cousyn* (Stroud, 2009)

Barnardiston, K.W., *Clare Priory* (Cambridge, 1962)

Bedingfield, H. & Gwynn-Jones, P., *Heraldry* (London, 1993)

Billson, C.J., *Mediaeval Leicester* (Edgar Backus, Leicester, 1920)

Blair, J. and Ramsey, N., eds, *English Medieval Industries* (London, 1991)

The History of King Richard the Third by Sir George Buck, Master of the Revels ed. A.N. Kincaid (Gloucester, 1979)

Butler, J., *The Quest for Becket's Bones* (London, 1995)

Carson, A.J., *Richard III: The Maligned King* (Stroud, 2008/2009, rev. edn 2013)

Carte, Rev. Samuel, *An Essay on the Antiquities and History of Leicester* (1721)

Carte, Thomas, *General History of England* (1747-55)

Cheetham, A., *The Life and Times of Richard III* (London, 1972)

Cox, J.C., *Memorials of Old Derbyshire* (London, 1907)

The Crowland Chronicle Continuations: 1459-1486, ed. N. Pronay and J. Cox (London, 1986)

Cunningham, S., *Richard III A royal enigma* (The National Archives, 2003)

Drake, Francis, *Eboracum* (London, 1736)

Edwards, R., *The Itinerary of King Richard III 1483-1485* (London, 1983, 1995)

Fabyan, Robert, *The Concordaunce of Hystoryes* (1559)

Fr Gilbert, OFMCap, PhD, *What to see in Walsingham* (Walsingham, 1948)

Hall, Edward, *The Union of the Two Noble and Illustre Famelies of Lancastre and Yorke* (1548)

Halsted, C.A., *Richard III as Duke of Gloucester and King of England* (London, 1844, facs. Elibron Classics, 2006)

Hammond, P.W. & Sutton, A.F., *Richard III: The Road to Bosworth Field* (London, 1985)

Hanham, A., *Richard III and his Early Historians 1483-1535* (Oxford, 1975)

Holinshed's Chronicles of England, Scotland and Ireland, Vol. 3 (London, 1808)

Horrox, R., *Richard III: A Study of Service* (Cambridge, 1989)

Jones, M.K., *Bosworth 1485: Psychology of a Battle* (Stroud, 2002)

Kendall P.M., *Richard III* (London, 1955)

Langley, P.J. and Jones, M.K. *The King's Grave: The Search for Richard III* (London, 2013)

The Itinerary of John Leland in or about the years 1535-1543, ed. L. Toulmin Smith (London, 1907)

Little, A.G., *The Greyfriars in Oxford* (Clarendon Press, 1892)

Martin, A., *Franciscan Architecture in England*, British Society for Franciscan Studies 18 (Manchester: The University Press, 1937)

Marks, R. & Payne, A., *Writhe's Garter Book*

Melhuish, J.M., *The College of King Richard III Middleham* (issued by permission of the Richard III Society)

Morris, M., Buckley, R. & Codd, M., *Visions of Ancient Leicester* (ULAS, 2011)

Nichols, J., *Bibliotheca Topographica Britannica*, No. 7 (London, 1782)

Nichols, J., *The History and Antiquities of the County of Leicester* (London, 1795-1811, 1815)

Petre, J., ed., *Richard III: Crown and People* (Gloucester, 1985)

Potter, J., *Good King Richard?* (London, 1983)

Ross, C., *Richard III* (London, 1981)

Rous, John, *Historia Johannis Rossi Warwicensis de Regibus Anglie*, ed. Thomas Hearne (Oxford, 1716) de Ruvigny, M.A.H.D., *The Plantagenet Roll of the Blood Royal*, 5 vols (London, 1903-1911)

Sandford, Francis, *A Genealogical History of the Kings of England* (London, 1677)

Skillington, S.H., *The Manor of Peckleton*, (W. Thornley & Son, Leicester, 1932)

Speede [Speed], J., *The History of Great Britaine* (London, 1611, 1614)

Stevens, J., *The History of the antient abbey, monasteries, hospitals, cathedral and collegiate churches* (London, 1722)

Sutton, A.F. & Visser-Fuchs, L., *The Hours of Richard III* (Stroud, 1996 edn)

Sutton, A.F., Visser-Fuchs, L. & Hammond, P.W., *The Reburial of Richard Duke of York, 21-30 July 1476* (London, 1991)

Tanner, T., *Notitia Monastica* (London, 1744)

Throsby, J., *History and Antiquities of the Ancient Town of Leicester* (J. Brown, Leicester, 1791)

Tolley, T., *A Book of Hours* (London, 1993)

Vergil, Polydore, *Anglica Historia* (1555), Lib. XXV (http://www.philological.bham.ac.uk/polverg/25lat.html)

Wagner, A.R., *The Records and Collections of the College of Arms* (London, 1951)

Watson, R., *Illuminated Manuscripts and their Makers* (London, 2003)

Weever, John, *Ancient Funeral Monuments* (London, 1631)

Wilkinson, J., *Richard: The Young King To Be* (Stroud, 2008)

Wren, C., *Parentalia, or Memoirs of the Family of the Wrens* (London, 1750)

Wright, K., *The Field of Bosworth* (Leicester, 2002)

York Records, Extracts from the Municipal Records of the City of York, ed. R. Davies (London, 1843, repr. 1976)

BL.MS Harl. 541 (*The Frowyk Chronicle, 1482-87*)

BL.MS Harl. 542 (*The Ballad of Bosworth Feilde*)

BL Add. MS 27879

BL Add. MS 45131

BL Cott. MS Vespasian FXIII

College of Arms MS I 3

TNA:PRO C1/206/69

Author Biographies

John Ashdown-Hill, BA Hons, MA, PhD, FSA, FRHistS
Historical researcher, writer and lecturer; the leader of genealogical research and historical adviser on the 'LOOKING FOR RICHARD' project, which led to the rediscovery of the remains of Richard III in August 2012. In recognition of this he was recently awarded an honorary second doctorate by the University of Essex. The research for his earlier PhD in history centred upon the client network of John Howard, Duke of Norfolk, in North Essex and South Suffolk. Since 1997 he has regularly given historical talks and published historical research, achieving a certain reputation in aspects of late mediaeval history. His publications include six books, five of which are focused on the late Middle Ages, and he has three more books on fifteenth-century history due out in 2015. He has participated in British and foreign television documentaries on Richard III, and a forthcoming Channel 4 documentary on the fate of the 'Princes in the Tower'.

Annette Carson
Having originally studied at the Royal College of Music, her career included working as a TV Organiser for British Equity, Programme Manager for Thames TV, and in PR and advertising as an award-winning copywriter. A freelance author with a preference for history and biography, she has sold over 46,000 non-fiction books on subjects including aviation and music, writes articles and has contributed to *Encyclopædia Britannica*. Her history of aerobatics was awarded the Tissandier Diploma of the Fédération Aéronautique Internationale. With a lifelong interest in Richard III, in 2008 she published *Richard III: The Maligned King* which led Philippa Langley to invite her to join the 'LOOKING FOR RICHARD' project as a historical consultant. In 2013 she published a short paperback (and eBook), *Richard III: A Small Guide to the Great Debate*, aimed at explaining the controversy to the general reader.

David Johnson BA Hons, MA, PhD
Wendy Johnson
Dr David and Wendy Johnson are long standing members of the Richard III Society and frequent contributors to the Society's quarterly journal the *Ricardian Bulletin*. David, whose PhD in history was awarded by the University of York in 2013, is the author of *Adwalton Moor 1643: The Battle That Changed A War* (Blackthorn Press, 2003), and Wendy has sold and exhibited portraits of people and animals. David is preparing a new study exploring the political controversy surrounding Richard III's accession to the throne, whilst Wendy is currently researching a proposed trilogy based on the Wars of the Roses.

Philippa Langley
A screenwriter and producer, Philippa Langley inaugurated the 'LOOKING FOR RICHARD' project and led the successful search to locate King Richard III's grave. She is a TAPS writer, a BAFTA Rocliffe shortlisted writer, and finalist in SWF's *Scriptmarket* and Channel 4's *'Son of the Pitch'* competition. Her 90 minute documentary, *The King in the Car Park*, made with Channel 4 and Darlow Smithson Productions, was Channel 4's highest rated specialist factual show, going on to win the Royal Television Society Award for 2013 and a BAFTA nomination in 2014. Her screenplay *Richard III: Last of the Warrior Kings* on the life of Richard III is based on *Bosworth 1485: Psychology of a Battle* by military historian Michael Jones, with whom she co-authored *The King's Grave: The Search for Richard III* in 2013. Founder of the Richard III Society's Scottish Branch, she is a regular contributor to the *Ricardian Bulletin* magazine and was awarded the Society's Robert Hamblin Award in 2012.

Index